My Magic Lights

Copyright © 2015 Peggy Weber

All rights reserved. All rights reserved in all media. No part of this book may be used or reproduced without written permission, by the author, except in the case of brief quotations embodied in critical articles and reviews.

The moral right of Peggy Weber as the author of this work has been asserted by her in accordance with the Copyright Designs, and Patents Act of 1988.

Published in the United Kingdom.

ISBN-13: 978-1502802491

CONTENTS

		Page:
1	*Earliest Memories*	1
2	*Never Be Frightened Said Mammy*	13
3	*I Was The Happiest Proudest Girl In All The World*	18
4	*I Was Dragged Under The Swirling Water*	26
5	*England Seemed A Very Long Way Away*	36
6	*Daddy's Idea Of An Emergency Wasn't The Same As Mine*	43
7	*Tony Looked So Handsome In His Grey Suit*	51
8	*I'd Catch A Bright Globe Like A Shimmering Bubble*	59
9	*I've Got A Present For You Babe, Said Tony, Proudly*	69
10	*Instantly I Was Transported Back to The Riverbank In Ireland*	81
11	*So What Is An Orb?*	94
12	*Evidence Orbs & My Questions Answered Through The Lens*	100
13	*The Grand Children Race with their Grandad*	109
14	*Sacred Sites*	116
15	*Journey From Orbs To Healing*	125
16	*Misty Images*	133

My Magic Lights

Dedication

With Special Thanks

Acknowledgements

✯✯✯✯

Testimonials

Summary

About the Author

IN DEDICATION TO....

In dedication to my wonderful Mother and Grandmother both of whom guided me well, from such a young age, at the start of what would become my spiritual journey.

Also, my dear Dad for teaching me how to use my spiritual insight wisely and always in an honourable way.

My wonderful husband and soul mate Tony, from whom I learned a lot about true love and of course, I especially dedicate this book to our four wonderful children, Teresa, Pat, Paul and Phil and our fantastic Grandchildren too, Charlie, George, Jaide, Danielle, Ruby and Tony.

Last but not least, in dedication to our very much missed and loved family members now in spirit, but clearly still with us!

WITH SPECIAL THANKS.....

Upon discussing the possibility of writing this book and not knowing where to start, I was introduced to a lovely lady called Linda Dearsley. During our first meeting, Linda filled me in on her background and casually produced one of the books she had written for 'Doris Stokes' (famous professional medium of the 1970's/80's. Doris was also the first ever medium to appear at the London Palladium, with ticket sales sold out within two hours).

After a very interesting meeting, when Linda had left, I had the feeling to try and communicate with Doris in spirit. In my mind, being introduced to Linda was no coincidence and I had a strong feeling that with the help of higher powers, Doris had helped put Linda in my path!

As a thank you, I just had to place Doris's book 'Voices in my Ear' on the chair and take a photo to see what I would get.

This resulting photo on the next page and just blew us away!

What a wonderful sign I had been given.

Linda is now a dear friend and I can't thank her enough for all her hard work, guidance and support she has given me in getting my own book produced!

Incredibly, the clear image inside this orb, is the outline of a person. during the first discussion to write a book about my spiritual experiences in collaboration with Linda Dearsley, could this seemingly be the image of Doris Stokes?......

Too many coincidences for it to be a coincidence perhaps.

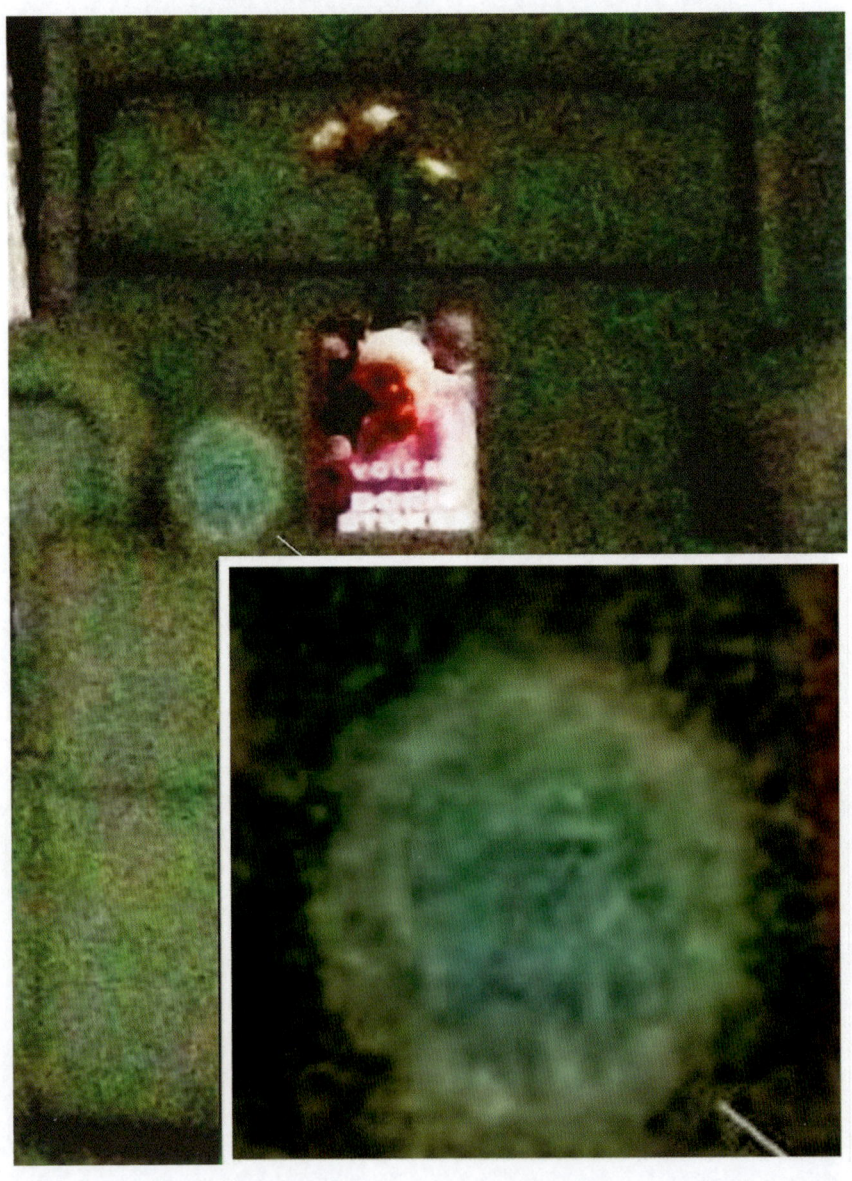

ACKNOWLEDGEMENTS

With special thanks to my daughter Pat for the production and design of 'My Magic Lights.' With the support of both Linda Dearsley, for helping me to get my life story written and my daughter Pat, for the many, sometimes frustrating hours putting this book together. This journey had been a lot longer and tougher than we thought, but it really has been a labour of love too!

Also, not forgetting my dear brother Michael Nealis, who I sincerely thank for his unwavering support over the years. Michael, also took the lovely photo of the bridge where we grew up, used on the front cover.

We had many great laughs out late at night with 'the lads' during our trips when taking photos in the pitch black to see what we would get!

∞CHAPTER 1∞

EARLIEST MEMORIES

It was an exciting day! I was four years old and we were moving out of my grandmother's cottage for the very first time and into a home of our own, a brand new council house, in the nearby village of Ballyragget, Kilkenny.

Mammy piled up the big old Silvercross pram with our belongings and off we went down Cool Lane and into Moate Road, me and my younger brother Richard, holding tightly to the side of the pram.

Mammy was in a happy mood as we trundled briskly along, the old pram springs squeaking over the pot holes, with my brown-ribboned plaits bouncing off my shoulders and Richard's little feet running to keep up. Past the sugar beet fields where Mammy often worked, we went on, beside the green meadow with a huge grey water tower in it.

Up and up into the sky, the water tower rose and my wondering four year old eyes went up and up towards the clouds with it. Then I gasped, my feet dragged and I let go of the pram. All around the top of the tower were the loveliest lights with lifelike people, a man in rich red robes with some sort of head-dress on his head, a woman in a beautiful blue gown with a veil on her head and other brightly coloured people all hovering around the top of the building like glorious glowing butterflies! 'Oh Mammy, look at all the lovely people on top of the tower'. I said. Mammy looked warily from me to the top of the tower and back again. 'Where?' 'Up there, on top of the tower', I said, pointing. 'There is a man and a lady and lots of others, some standing, and some kneeling down like this'. I dropped down on my knees in the dust to imitate them.

Mammy pulled me up and put my hand firmly back on the pram. 'Now that's enough Peg', she said. 'Come on, pick your feet up and not a word to anyone, do you hear?' And on we went again, with me looking back over my shoulder at the lovely people, until the water tower disappeared from sight.

A few weeks later, now settled into our new home, Mammy took my brother Richard and I to the local Church. Christmas was approaching and a nativity scene had been set up in front of the altar. A donkey and some dear little sheep immediately attracted my eye. Then I noticed the other figures standing with them in the straw. 'Oh look Mammy!!', I cried in delight, 'that's the people from the top of the tower', except they were not moving in the Church like they were in the tower and later on I knew these to be nativity characters.

'Whished' (sshhhush) Peg for heaven's sake!' said Mammy, 'The Priest'll hear you.'

You didn't argue with Mammy, so I bit my lip, but it was difficult as there were so many things you weren't supposed to talk about.

I was born Margaret Nealis on July 10th 1944, the oldest of thirteen surviving children, born to my Mother Bridget and my Father Hubert. (Poor Mammy had seventeen children I am told, but lost four). The story goes that we were originally called 'McNealis', but my grandad was so afraid of the 'Banshee', the legendary Irish wailing ghost - that he changed the family name. Apparently, according to ancient Folklore, legend has it, the Banshee followed all those with the name 'Mac' and if her awful howling cry was ever heard, one family member would die within three days!

My grandfather was so scared of the Banshee following him, that he dropped the 'Mac', from his name to throw her off the scent and we became the 'Nealis' family from then on. It seemed to have worked, as none of us ever heard the Banshee!

For some reason, Daddy never called me Margaret, but always Peg and that name stuck too. But then we had a lot of nick names in our family. Mammy was known as 'Diddle' ever since Daddy bought a little apron home from the army, which had little characters on the front depicting the famous nursery rhyme, 'Hey Diddle, Diddle, the Cat and the Fiddle', when the cow jumped over the moon. I expect he jokingly shouted out at Mammy the name 'Diddle' and that stuck too! Richard became Dick and my grandparents were lovingly known as Muddy and Daddy Cool, because they lived in Cool lane. Though her real name was Bridie and his was Ned.

Daddy was a sergeant in the Army and lived away initially at the army base in Kildare. He later moved on to Custom Barracks, Athlone, Co Westmeath. So for our first few years, Mammy, Dick and I lived in Cool Lane with Muddy and Daddy Cool in their tiny thatched cottage, a few miles from the village. It was idyllic and surrounded by lilac trees and climbing plants with a little vegetable patch.

There was no electricity or running water and one of my earliest memories was of Dick and I, when we were very small being put by the fire in two old fashioned tea chests to use as play pens, Dick in one and me in the other. Of course, there were no such things as play pens back then and in those parts this was the norm! No one had much furniture and tea chests were a highly adaptable and valued alternative. Upturned, they served as bedside stands and of course you could also store things in them. As young children, at least Mammy knew where we were, as we couldn't move out of them!

I will always remember the glow of the open fire bouncing off the furniture on to the walls. But Muddy also had two Tillie lamps on the wall and an oil lamp on the table. Over the big old fireplace hung her pride and joy, a picture of the Queen Mother, taken from the centre pages of the newspaper and in colour. The photograph showed the Queen Mother sitting down wearing a lovely light blue dress and a diamond tiara. Muddy Cool put it in a frame and hung it there beside her Brigid Cross. Everyone had small Brigid Crosses (woven from rushes) on the wall. They were believed to protect the house from fire.

Grandmother came from a Romany family. They never spoke about it as grandad wasn't Romany, but some evenings we'd walk up to Muddy's to find dozen's of brown and white horses trotting down the hill pulling colourful caravans, vibrantly painted in bright reds, blues and gold's and hung with various swinging saucepans and pans. They would draw up outside Muddy's and the ladies would get out. It struck me they were all wearing black dresses and jumpers with holes in them, despite their colourful homes.

Muddy Cool would come out to see them and they would climb the bank beside the cottage, move aside the empty milk churns from the old stone slab, where the farmers kept them and lay out cake and drinks on the flat surface. Then the men would fetch accordions and spoons and play music whilst the ladies sat around chatting. Couples danced rapid jigs in the deserted road and I would slip away to stroke the horses, quietly grazing on the grass. I loved it when Muddy's relatives came to visit.

Maybe it was because she was Romany at heart, or just because her kitchen was so small, but Muddy Cool liked doing things outside. She did her washing in a big barrel tub on the grass with a wooden wash board and she also cooked outdoors. She lit a fire and made rabbit stew in the heavy round pot that hung over the flames.

Between stews, that pot became a bread oven. Muddy stoked up the fire, put dough in the pot, turned the lid upside down and scooped some of the burning coals in to the lid as well, so there was heat from above and heat from below and soon the aroma of baking bread filled the air, making our mouths' water unbearably. The loaves always came out steaming, delicious and perfectly round.

Muddy always wandered the fields collecting apples for pies and cakes, nettles to use as green vegetables or to make into tea and wild mushrooms. One day she was making a stew with a pile of mushrooms she'd picked when she held out two of them for me.

'Can you tell which one is different Peg?' she asked. I looked at them carefully. At first they looked exactly the same but I knew there must be something different about them or she wouldn't have asked. Then I noticed that one of them was a funny colour inside. 'That's right,' said Muddy, 'If you see that in the field, you don't touch it.'

Looking back now I think Muddy was very psychic. There were always people coming to the cottage and sitting around a big pot of tea. Then after a while they'd throw the tea out. And I thought – why are they coming for a cup of tea then throwing it away instead of drinking it?! But, of course now I realise they were having their tea leaves read.

There was also what I thought to be a mysterious round stone that Muddy and my aunts passed between them and quickly covered up if anyone came near. Why they spent so much time staring at a stone I couldn't think, but now I believe it must have been a crystal ball.

Grandmother's son Uncle Neddy, whose real name was of course Edward, was a real character and a great favourite with us children. He was full of fun, always playing tricks and jumping out at you when you weren't expecting it. You always knew when Uncle Neddy was coming down the road because he'd be singing or humming his favourite tune 'Home, home on the Range' and you'd catch a few lines of 'Where the deer and the antelope play...' threading towards you on the breeze before Neddy came into view.

Uncle Neddy lived at Muddy Cool's his whole life. He was in love with a girl named Nell Cane from the down the road – a slender young woman with elegant dresses that swished around her slim calves, strappy sandals and hair swept up like Lucille Ball's. Nell was in love with Neddy too but their parents wouldn't allow them to get married, so Neddy remained a bachelor for the rest of his days.

Neddy was a natural talent as an artist and painted wonderful country scenes, but he made his living cutting turf and his face and hands were usually stained black with peat. But Neddy didn't just cut turf, he and his friend Davey used to go out poaching too. In the dead of the night, they'd catch salmon from the river and rabbits from the meadows and they'd help themselves to potatoes and turnips from the farmer's fields too.

Then they'd go round the village discreetly handing out the much needed food to families who were struggling – and there were plenty of those. Mammy was often a grateful recipient and some dark nights I'd look out the bedroom window and wonder why Uncle Neddy was digging holes in the garden and filling them with straw. I realize now of course it was to hide the stolen potatoes and turnips and keep them in good condition in the cold weather.

One Christmas Eve we were full of excitement and reluctant to go to bed but Uncle Neddy said, 'If you're quiet now and go to bed nicely, leaving the curtains open – as long as you stay in bed, I reckon you'll see Santa fly past the window because it's a bright Moon'.

So we drew back the curtains and went to bed and waited and waited, staring out at the dark sky. We could see the stars and the bright moonlight just as Uncle Neddy had predicted. And then suddenly, there was a noise somewhere outside and Santa's smiling face appeared at the window. Right at the glass as if he was looking in at us! Clear as clear we saw his red hat, white beard, rosy nose and beaming grin – then he crossed the window, still beaming and was gone – no doubt to visit other children on his Christmas rounds. We were squealing with excitement. For the first time ever, we'd actually seen Santa! It made our Christmas.

It was to be years before we found out how he did it. Uncle Neddy had somehow got hold of a Santa mask and fixed it onto the end of a long broom handle. Then he'd gone out into the garden, held it up to our window and walked the mask past so that Santa's face moved right across our glass and then flew away into the night. Magic!

Somehow Uncle Neddy always managed to be around when there was mischief going on. One day Dick and I and a few friends had sneaked off school to go scrumping for nuts in a farmer's field. I was the best climber – a real tomboy. If I could climb something, the others would know it was safe to follow – so of course this particular day I was the one at the top of the tree, shaking the nuts down to the children beneath who were cracking them open and sharing them round. The ground under the tree was carpeted in broken shells and of course Uncle Neddy was in there gathering up the nuts with the rest of them.

Suddenly I looked out from the tree and saw an awful sight. Oh Jesus, it was Mammy coming across the fields towards us and she was rolling her sleeves up, her mouth set in a tight, angry line. How she found out I'll never know. Panicking, I looked around for another exit but the alternative escape route was through a field with a bull in it.

I'd stopped shaking the tree in my horror and Uncle Neddy, glancing up to see what was wrong spotted Mammy too. 'Well kids, your Mother's coming', he said. 'It looks like you either face the bull or your Mammy and I tell you now, if it was me, I'd rather face the bull!'

We understood how he felt, but on looking at the huge dark beast with its small mean eyes and a ring through the nose decided it was just too much for us! I slid down the tree and we waited meekly, nut shells crunching under our feet for Mammy to arrive and haul us home. We got a wallop, a telling off and we were marched back in disgrace – but of course it didn't stop us skiving off school the next time.

The new council house we'd been allocated was in a cul-de-sac within a row of terrace houses near the centre of Ballyragget. It had a long front garden and three bedrooms. All the boys slept in one room and the girls in another. No one had their own bed. In the village no child had their own room or bed.

Each bedroom contained one large bed and eventually the girl's room housed five of us sisters sleeping three at the top and two at the bottom. On cold winter nights, Mammy put bricks in the fire to heat them up, and then wrapped them up in towels to put in the bed to keep us warm.

We didn't think of ourselves as poor; we were just like everyone else but life must have been a struggle for Mammy and Daddy. Daddy sent money back from his army base but it wasn't enough, so Mammy had to work too. She worked in the fields, picking potatoes and thinning beet - hard back breaking work. She used to come back soaking wet, really drenched to the skin. Even as a child it broke my heart to see her come home so chilled and shivering. She developed arthritis in her hands, knees and feet but she still had to carry on.

Yet, even then it was difficult to make ends meet. Nothing was wasted. Newspapers were turned into toilet paper. Our knitted jumpers would be unravelled as soon as we grew out of them and were re-knitted over and over again, for smaller and smaller jumpers and eventually to be made into cushion covers.

Toys were more or less unheard of. The occasional child might have had a little doll or a train but mostly we didn't expect toys or presents. There was no toy shop in the village and it wouldn't have occurred to us to ask for anything. At Christmas we were happy to find an apple, an orange and a bit of chocolate in the socks we hung up over the fireplace for Santa.

Yet we were never bored. The village was full of big families and there were always children to play with in the street. Horses ruled the road then and there was little traffic. We marked out squares with bits of chalk and played hopscotch; we raced and chased up the lane and our Mother's washing lines were in big demand as skipping ropes. My friend Frances, (from across the road) and I were always borrowing Mammy's washing line to tie round the gate post so that the two of us could skip.

There were always trees to climb or swing from and the river to paddle in or fish for minnows.

Then there was the game of postmen and parcels. That was one of our favourites. Most homes, however bare could manage to obtain a small statue of a protective saint to bring good luck to the household. Mammy had a little statue of St. Theresa in beige and brown robes, which she kept in a cupboard and Frances's Mammy, had an ornate model called the 'Child of Prague'. Secretly, I liked the Child of Prague much better than our dowdy St. Theresa, as he wore splendid red and gold robes and had a little crown on his head.

Anyway Frances and I would borrow the family saints and make them into parcels by wrapping them in old scraps of brown paper tied with string. Then we'd play postmen and deliver them to each other's houses.

Somehow the Child of Prague usually ended up in our house and St. Theresa was delivered to Frances's home. Often it wasn't long before our mothers came out and the parcels had to be swapped back again but occasionally they wouldn't notice. Then weeks later from Frances's home would come the cry: 'That's not my ornament!' Or Mammy would go to the cupboard to find red and gold robes, a minute crown and the beady little eyes of the Child of Prague staring back at her. 'That's not my statue Peg!' she'd shout and of course plainly dressed St. Theresa would have to be retrieved.

Food was often a problem. Mammy would make huge pans of porridge which we ate for breakfast and sometimes tea too, with a drop of milk and a sprinkle of sugar. Other days there was bread for breakfast with sugar, or for a real treat, spread with dripping. When meat was available we had a pig's head, split down the middle, so there were two parts. We also had cow's tongue, kidneys and liver. Of course if Uncle Neddy got us a rabbit, Mammy made rabbit stew.

I'll never forget one Christmas when someone had given Mammy a goose to fatten. She'd fattened that goose as best she could for months before until finally Christmas Eve arrived and Mickey Caldey – (who did these things for the village), was called in to kill it.

So Mickey arrived, carrying a pillow case. He was escorted to the goose and to our surprise, put the pillow case over the goose's head so it wouldn't see what was happening. But the goose must have sensed something amiss, panicked and ran off down the garden with just its little orange legs sticking out the bottom of the flapping fabric.

We watched in amazement from our bedroom window as Mickey roared off down the garden after the animated pillow case and then Mammy suddenly appeared waving a meat cleaver and roared off down the garden after Mickey. Struck by an unexpected pang of remorse for the goose, she'd changed her mind.

'You touch that goose Mickey Caldey and I'll take your head off!' She shouted as she ran. 'But Diddle!' protested Mickey, 'You asked me to come down and kill the goose'. 'I tell you now; if you touch that goose I'll kill you!' Yelled Mammy.

So the goose was spared, we had pigs trotters for Christmas dinner that year and none of us minded a bit.

But sometimes, particularly in the summer, there was no food at all.

'Right the lot of ye', Mammy said, 'it's the fields for you today, we've got nothing to eat'.

So out we went into the fields hunting for wild strawberries, blackberries, mushrooms, dandelion leaves and even the odd egg a hen might have laid in the hedgerow and forgotten about. Any eggs were carefully wrapped in our hankies. Mushrooms and fruit we threaded onto long pieces of dried grass, like wild kebabs and we carried them home for Mammy to share out. The lane was like a pantry to us.

Being outdoors so much was normal for country children in Ireland in those days. It made us very close to nature. I think that's why so many legends abounded in that part of the world. We could sense magic, all around us.

It was in the air. We took it for granted that unseen beings shared our land. As well as the banshee, we believed in fairies that flitted around, just beyond our sight, along with their mischievous companions, the leprechauns.

We knew all about leprechauns and their fabled pots of gold. Often we trotted down the field hoping to find a pot of gold left in the ditch - but there never was.

Yet I wasn't too disappointed because it wasn't long before I found my own private magic.

∞CHAPTER 2∞

'NEVER BE FRIGHTENED,' SAID MAMMY...

Down on the riverbank the light was beginning to fade, the shadows under the old stone bridge were deepening and one by one the other children were drifting home for tea.

But I was still catching minnows in a jam jar and besides, it was one of those afternoons when I knew it just wasn't worth rushing home. There was next to nothing to eat and I hated to see the sad look in Mammy's eyes when she hadn't enough food to fill our hungry stomachs.

'Are you coming Peg?' asked Frances. 'In a bit.' I said, 'You go on. I won't be long.'

So Frances gathered up her things, climbed back over the gate, out onto the old road and was gone. I was alone with just the sound of the water trickling over the stones and the wind in the trees. Alone, yet I wasn't lonely and I certainly didn't feel nervous. There was a calm, friendly feel about the river bank. I lay on my stomach in the grass, dreamily trailing the jam jar through the clear water, humming a little tune to myself.

And then something bright caught my eye. I glanced up. There on the opposite bank a tiny pink light was twinkling. As I watched, it skittered to the side and then another light appeared - a little green dot of colour. I sat up, intrigued. Goodness knows what they were but as I stared, more and more lights began to blossom. Red, blue, yellow - tiny lights like you saw on Christmas trees but dancing and weaving through the air.

Entranced, I just sat there and watched them perform their aerial ballet as the sun went down and the sky got darker and darker. Heaven knows how long I stayed. But after a while the lights began to move away and I realized the damp was coming up from the grass, making my legs cold.

Mammy must be wondering where I'd got to.

So I jumped up and ran home, replaying the magical scene over and over again in my mind. I didn't say anything about it to anyone - instinctively I knew not to talk about it. But after that I went down to the river on my own as often as I could, to see the magic lights. And they never failed me. As long as I was alone, one by one the beautiful lights returned. 'My magic lights' I called them - it felt as though they were putting on their wonderful show just for me and to bring me comfort.

Looking back, I must have seemed a quiet child, a bit reserved and shy. I was always in a little world of my own, despite my tomboy climbing skills.

I saw things that were puzzling. Sometimes there'd be a child running down the road, a child I didn't recognize and then somehow, they just weren't there anymore. No matter how I climbed the field gates and peered around looking for them or stared into neighbours' gardens, there was no sign. They just disappeared into thin air. Other times, they'd be standing by a bush, smiling at me as if inviting me to play but as soon as I took a step forward, they vanished.

One day I mentioned it to Muddy Cool but she didn't seem at all surprised.

'Don't worry about it Peg,' she said calmly as if it was the most natural thing in the world, 'and never be frightened, but don't tell anyone at school.'

Then there was the time there was a big funeral in the village and we all went to the graveyard. It was a dull, rainy day but I was curious. There were so many people and most of them were crying. 'Mammy why is everyone crying?' I asked. Mammy sighed. 'You see that lovely wooden box over there?' she said, pointing to the place where there seemed to be a big hole in the ground and a group of men lowering a long, thin box into it, while the priest stood there saying prayers. I nodded. Of course I saw it. 'Well, they are saying goodbye to their Mammy as she is inside that box. That's why they're crying.'

I was even more puzzled now. 'No she's not.' I said, 'She's over there by the gate with those other people.'

There she was, plain as plain, standing on the edge of a group of people near the entrance to the graveyard, wearing a blue dress and with a handbag over her arm, as normal as can be and smiling over at me.

'Look Mammy! There she is, just there!' I said pointing helpfully. 'She's not in that box.'

Mammy pushed my arm down quickly. 'Whshhhhed,' she hissed, 'Be quiet!' She was afraid someone would tell the priest.

But I just couldn't understand about death or see any sadness in it. Not long after this came the news that Uncle Neddy's brother, my Uncle Billy who had apparently gone to work on the railways in England had been killed in an accident.

I remember the day they brought his body home. I was out in the street skipping and I saw this big black hearse coming slowly up the road with lots of people walking behind it. 'Stop skipping!' snapped Mammy, hurrying over, 'That's your Uncle in there.'

So I stopped skipping and we stood there side by side, watching respectfully as the hearse went mournfully by. Yet my understanding of what had happened wasn't quite the same as everyone else's.

Late that night I slipped out of the house and walked down our long front path to sit on the step by the gate. It was very cold and the lane was glistening with ice but the sky was clear, the stars pin sharp whilst the large moon shone brilliantly bright. I stared up at it, carefully, searching the silvery surface.

'Peg!' shouted Mammy, 'Whatever are you doing out there? 'Come in and shut the door - it's freezing!'

'I can't Mammy,' I shouted back, 'I'm waiting for Uncle Billy to wave down from the Moon.'

Mammy wasn't having any of that. Despite the fact that Uncle Billy had yet to make an appearance, she marched me back inside, firmly shut the door and sent me up to bed with a fire-baked brick wrapped in a towel to warm my frozen feet.

It wasn't that Mammy didn't believe me, she plainly did. Often when I was playing she'd call me over: 'Peg come over here. What do you see?' and I'd have to describe a scene that was clear as day to me but for some reason she couldn't see it.

We often had strange noises in the house, though it wasn't particularly old and doors would open and close on their own. This was more annoying than frightening.

'Peg, the door's open again,' Mammy would say as we sat by the fire, so I'd get up and shut it but a few minutes later it would come open again.

One evening I was alone in the sitting room when I distinctly heard the front door open and footsteps in the hall behind me. Yet I just knew if I looked round, there'd be no one there and even as the thought was going through my mind, the most wonderful feeling of peace and happiness flowed into the room. I sat quite still, not wanting to break the spell. Behind me the invisible feet began to climb the stairs. I could hear them quietly moving from step to step and as they neared the top, I couldn't resist turning to look.

As I got to the door I was just in time to catch a glimpse of a golden boot disappearing round the stair post on the landing. Yet of course, once I got upstairs, there was no one there.

∞CHAPTER 3∞

I WAS THE HAPPIEST, PROUDEST GIRL IN ALL THE WORLD

Daddy was a fine looking man, tall and strong with black hair and kind, warm twinkly eyes. I was so proud of him. He was away a lot at the army base in Custom Barracks, Athlone. From being away, he would come home in his smart sergeant's uniform with shiny buttons. He was so handsome, I felt like I'd burst with pride just skipping down the street at his side.

It was always a red letter day the day Daddy came home on leave. Being the oldest, I used to find out when he would be arriving and I'd run off to the railway station on my own to meet his train, without telling the others, so I could have him all to myself for a few precious minutes. The trains were steam trains in those days so I'd stand on the platform for ages and ages, staring up the line for the first faint smudge of smoke on the horizon that told me the engine was approaching.

For a while after the war we used to receive occasional parcels from some distant relatives in the United States. They sent warm clothes and odds and ends that their children had grown out of and we were very glad of them.

One day a parcel arrived containing an elegant blue hat with a tassel on. I was small for my age but it was just the right size for me and it went well with a little blue coat they'd sent in a previous package. I loved that hat and of course Daddy hadn't seen me in it yet, so the next time he was due home on leave, I dressed myself up, perched the fine hat on my head and ran to the station to watch out for the train. I was so excited. I wanted to show off I suppose. I couldn't wait for Daddy to see me in my new hat.

It seemed like hours but eventually a tell-tale plume of grey smoke appeared against the distant clouds, getting bigger and bigger until at last the huge engine puffed slowly into the station and screeched to a stop. The people climbed out, doors slammed, but to my horror, Daddy wasn't amongst them. Anxiously I scanned every face moving up the platform but there was no handsome sergeant in a gleaming uniform.

Then the guard blew his whistle, a huge cloud of steam hissed out, enveloping everything, the engine roared and the train began to chug away again in a thick fog.

I was so sad, so disappointed. I watched as the train moved slowly down the line, under the bridge and away. I watched until all that was left was a dense cloud of steam under the bridge. And then suddenly through the steam I could make out a dark shape, it was moving towards the platform, getting bigger and more distinct and as the mist thinned away I realised it was Daddy! He'd jumped out the carriage and hidden under the bridge to make me laugh.

Instant joy shot through me. He'd come after all! Delighted, I ran to him, and he picked me up and swung me round and I was the happiest, proudest girl in all the world. Daddy was home - and he thought I looked a picture in my new hat too.

When Daddy was home on leave, life seemed more exciting. Mammy was happy and the house was full of laughter. Daddy could do all sorts of unexpected things. Once, he showed me how to make his special trifle.

We went into the kitchen and he took out a bowl, broke up some bread into small pieces and laid them carefully in the bottom. Then he made a red jelly and poured it over the bread and we left the jelly to set.

A little later, back we went to the kitchen and Daddy made custard in a saucepan and showed me how to stand the saucepan in cold water when the custard was ready, to cool it down. Carefully he poured the cool custard over the jelly and finally he grated a little more bread into breadcrumbs, tossed them in a hot, dry frying pan to toast them and then scattered them over the top of the custard. It was absolutely delicious. So not only was Daddy home - but there was trifle too for tea. A big treat.

Daddy would walk around the village with us, greeting our neighbours and his old friends. He and Mammy went to the pub on Saturday nights where the men drank stout, the women had cups of tea and someone would strike up on a fiddle or accordion and everyone would dance.

And should he be home on St. Patrick's Day March 17 it was even more fun. Mammy sent us out the day before to pick shamrocks from the fields. We'd take them home in a bit of brown paper and put them in a jam jar of water overnight.

On the big day, the school was closed and everyone pinned shamrocks to their coats and headed through streets decked with green to the church for the St. Patrick's Day mass. First it was the solemn mass, then on the way home everyone stopped off at the pub - now a vision of emerald green - for more beer, tea, lemonade for the children and dancing. Later still there was a special St. Patrick's Day cake, in which for some reason, a ring was hidden, which was supposed to bring you good luck if it was in your slice. I got it once, which was very exciting but it had to go back at the end of the day.

Oddly enough, most of the time Daddy, and quite a few of the fathers, didn't come with us to church. It was never discussed, we just accepted that Mammy went to church and Daddy didn't. But Daddy used to say to me: 'Peg, never go into a church unless you want to and it doesn't matter which church you go into. If you want to go into it, go.'

As it happens I love old churches and years later I was walking into one when a woman said to me: 'Peg you shouldn't be going into that church. That's not a Catholic church'.

And Daddy's voice came back to me down the years and I said: 'It's a church isn't it? What does it matter?' and I went in.

But despite Daddy's reservations, the church played a big part in our lives. I liked going mainly because for me it was a treasure house of pretty things. I loved to see the statues, all colourful in their painted splendour – St. Patrick in green, Jesus in red robes, Mary in her blue dress and St. John in brown. Then there were the Stations of the Cross illustrated with a series of bright, biblical pictures and round the walls were old stained glass windows that lit up when the sun came out.

There was also the little drama of watching the rest of the congregation arrive. No one was allowed to enter the church until Lady Dowder from the big house with the very long drive near the station, had made her entrance. Even though it was the 1950's by then, Lady Dowder travelled in a carriage pulled by a horse. So we all stood outside, including the priest, until the horse clip-clopped up the road and the carriage drew up by the church.

Then the priest would step forward and open the carriage door and Lady Dowder, dressed in a floor length Victorian gown and an old bonnet tied up under her chin would be helped out and escorted slowly into the building. She moved very slowly did Lady Dowder but I suppose she must have been a very great age.

But while the church was a source of wonder to me, it must have been stressful for Mammy. She obviously lived in fear of my 'strange' ways coming to the attention of the priest because she 'whissshd' (sshhssed) me so often, and finding money for the weekly collection was a real struggle.

Every seven days a little brown envelope would be delivered to your home, with your street and house number written on the back of it - nothing anonymous about these donations. You were expected to put money in the envelope for the church, even if you didn't have money to put bread on the table. The envelope was picked up a few days later. It was a disgrace in those days if you couldn't find a few pennies at the very least to put in it.

Every Sunday the priest would stand up in front of the congregation and publicly shame anyone who'd failed to make their donation.

'We note that Mrs Nealis (or some other poor soul) didn't send back her envelope.' the priest would announce disapprovingly and everyone would glance over at the blushing culprit who was trying to look as if it must be some other Mrs Nealis he was referring to. How Mammy must have dreaded those Sundays when she knew she'd been unable to scrape up even a few coppers for the brown envelope.

Years later I went back to the church and noticed on a shelf a pile of brown envelopes identical to the ones that caused so much worry in our house. I picked one up, took a pen from my bag and wrote on it: 'I see there's no change here.' and left it on the pulpit.

The odd thing was that Mammy was fearless in every other way - mothers were tough then, they had to be. They stood up to everyone except the priest.

In our part of Ireland the police are called the Garda. Our village Garda was a horrible man - a fat bully with ginger hair and a peaked cap jammed onto his head. He loved to swagger up and down the streets around 'the barracks' as we called the police station but one day he came stomping down the terrace, opened our gate, banged on the front door and had the audacity to put one foot on Mammy's beautifully scrubbed doorstep. He'd come to complain about so mething - possibly he'd seen us scrumping apples.

But in Ballyragget if anyone went in past your front gate without invitation it was trespassing and Mammy wouldn't put up with it.

The front door flew open and the Garda was confronted by Mammy at her fiercest. 'You put the other foot on that step and see what you'll get!' she yelled, her eyes flashing fire.

Frances and I were skipping outside at the time and Frances went white as Mammy's words floated down to us. 'Oh no! Your Mammy's going to jail!' she said, horrified.

But Mammy didn't go to jail. The Garda hastily removed his foot from the step, back pedalled to a safe distance, huffed and puffed a bit and made as quick a getaway as his dignity would allow.

Mammy could see off the Garda without a thought but the priest was a different matter altogether.

Yet not all the clergymen were intimidating. Father Canon Moore who also looked after our village was revered. He was practically a saint. He was an old man with holes in his shoes, a little white dog that followed at his heels and a walking stick. Quite often, particularly in the winter, he'd pop into the village school to see how the children were getting on.

The school was run by nuns back then and we were all taught in one big room. It was freezing cold in winter and though there was a little fire going at the front of the classroom, the heat didn't reach the seats at the back.

Every day the children who could afford it brought sandwiches for lunch and milk, poured into empty lemonade bottles for morning break. When the weather was cold we'd stand the bottles of milk round the fire as we arrived, to warm them up for playtime.

Father Canon Moore would come in with his little dog and walking stick and he'd take his stick and slowly count the bottles round the fire. Then he'd turn and count the number of children in the class.

'Hands up those who didn't have milk?' he'd say and quite a few of us would put up our hands. 'Right,' he'd say, 'I'll come back soon.' And off he'd go to the local shop, Mickey and May Shea's and ask for milk. They'd tell him the price and he'd say: 'Oh go on! It's for little children...' and invariably they'd let him have the milk and often a few sweets as well, for nothing. Then he brought the bottles back and stood them by the fire with the others. No child went without milk when Father Canon Moore was around.

Our favourite teacher-nun was Sister Cecilia. She was lovely. She had a kind, gentle face and a soft voice and she was always patient with us. Sister Rosaria was the complete opposite however. I can only think she didn't like being a nun because she was so bad tempered and cruel. She had a red face, which probably looked redder against the white of her robe and if her angry eyes should settle on you, you knew you were in for it.

'Come here you!' she'd shout in her loud, bellowing way and just the sound of her voice made me tremble.

Once, out in the playground, I got a message that Sister Rosaria wanted to see me. I can't even remember what it was about now - some small incident that occurred during a game - but I was struck with such terror I could hardly move. I found Sister Cecilia and hid behind her skirts, hanging onto the rosary round her waist with tightly clenched fists. 'It's fine Peg. Don't worry,' said Sister Cecilia, prizing me gently out and unhooking my fingers 'come on, I'll come with you.'

And she took me to Sister Rosaria, explained the situation and everything was fine - just as she'd promised. But without her intercession who knows what might have happened. Sister

Rosaria was known to hit you at times with a ruler turned on its side to make it hurt more.

'Hold your hand out!' she'd bark, face turning redder than ever and even though you were freezing cold and hungry you'd have to hold your hand out and receive the blows without flinching.

But it could have been worse. There were rumours going round that sometimes girls who were not married somehow had babies and these babies were taken by the nuns and never seen again. It sounded unlikely to me. Maybe the story-tellers were getting confused with the Bible account of Mary and the Angel who came to tell her she was having a little son, despite not being married to Joseph at the time.

But whatever the truth of it, I kept as far away from Sister Rosaria as I could.

∞CHAPTER 4∞

'I WAS DRAGGED UNDER THE SWIRLING WATER....'

Wonderful as Daddy's visits home always were, there'd come a day when he'd have to announce: 'I'm going away again.' And we'd sigh and we were disappointed of course but there was also a touch of excitement too because this announcement meant it was time for the Cadbury's chocolate treasure hunt.

Since we seldom even had enough food to take a sandwich to school for lunch - most days we had to make do with just the milk Father Canon Moore obtained for us - chocolate was a rare treat. But every time he came home Daddy managed to lay his hands on several very large, family size bars of Cadbury's Dairy Milk. You didn't see great big chocolate bars like that very often in Ballyragget.

Before we were up in the morning, he must have gone out and hidden these bars deep in the grass along the railway track towards Muddy Cool's house and we were sent scampering off to find them - partly I suspect now, to give Daddy and Mammy some private time alone together before he left.

Sometimes we'd walk for half an hour before finding the first one. We'd dash on and on, scouring every bush, every clump of grass until at last there'd be a blissful flash of purple peeping out and we'd cry: 'I've found one, I've found one!' and snatch it up, tearing off the wrappings to reveal the wondrous slab of chocolate, studded with thick chunky brown squares.

I've loved that glorious shade of purple ever since. And of course, by the time we got home, happy and chocolate-smeared, Daddy would be gone. In fact his train probably passed us as we stumbled back, sharing out our treasure as we walked.

The railway line brought Daddy to us and it took him away again. It was also a handy route to our grandmother's house and sometimes, the line was used by us to play on as a playground. If people warned us not to play on it, I didn't remember it, and if they had, we certainly took no notice.

One day, scuffling about near the railway line we noticed one of those little four wheeled pump-cart wagons that go along the track - apparently abandoned on the line and just crying out to be used. So, just like in the silent movies, we climbed aboard and by pumping the lever up and down we found we could make it move.

'Let's go to Muddy Cool's!' we said.

So pumping madly and giggling at our efforts, we set off up the line. It was harder work than we thought but we were making good progress. What we'd forgotten though, was that the route took us right through the station where the station master was usually patrolling the platform. It would be difficult to get past without him noticing. But as we were pondering this problem and the station was approaching, we heard this loud, 'Whooo, whooo! whooo, whooo..!' behind us.

We looked round, and to our horror saw the steam train approaching the station from behind us. In a panic we tried to switch the cart to the other rail but somehow couldn't get across, so we pumped faster and faster, desperately trying to reach the station. The train was coming closer all the time, frantically hooting and up ahead we could see the bulky figure of the station master looming on the platform.

Somehow we made it to the station, the train squealed and slithered to a halt behind us and as the station master strode angrily over, we leapt off the cart and galloped away.

'You little 'devils!' We heard him shouting behind us, 'Come here!' But of course that only made us run faster. We got clean away - but it was quite a while before we dared show our faces at the station again.

Despite this, in those days when there were very few cars on the roads, we had a fascination with transport. In the summer at harvest time we took big cans of tea down to the lads in the fields. It was thirsty, back-breaking work cutting the hay by hand in the blazing sun all day and they laboured from dawn till dusk, so they were very glad of our refreshments.

I loved going down to see them. The hay would be lying around the field all golden and sweet-smelling and the huge shire horses stood patiently by the wagons, flanks gleaming, just waiting to take it away to Kilkenny.

One day Dick, my friend Betty Ryan and I noticed that one of the wagons was all loaded, ready to go. The hay was piled so high that if we hung onto the back of the wagon, the farmer sitting at the front holding the reigns, couldn't see us. He had no idea in fact that we were there. So, just as he was setting off, we jumped onto the back of the cart and hung onto the rough wooden bars, hay tickling our faces all the way to Kilkenny, several miles up the bumpy road.

The farmer was furious when we arrived and he found us clinging there, rather dusty and red faced by now. But he was a good man. 'Just stay there while I unload!' he ordered, 'I'm going to take you back.'

So we had to wait while he unloaded all the hay and then we were ordered into the empty wagon and sat up there, feeling grand amongst the wisps of scattered straw, as we were driven back to Ballyragget by two splendid shire horses. If we were meant to be in disgrace, it didn't feel like it!

Looking back, we were lucky to escape from our adventures unharmed. It really did seem sometimes as if we had a guardian angel watching over us. I remember once going down to the river, on my own as usual, to see the magic lights but for some reason they didn't arrive immediately.

I wandered about for a bit watching the water flowing by. Then I slipped off my shoes and paddled up and down.

Further upstream, just under the bridge was a place we were absolutely forbidden to go near. The river did something strange there. You could see it if you hung over the parapet and looked down. There was a spot where the water went round and round in circles, very fast. Rather like the way the water swirled round and round the plug hole in the sink at home before disappearing down the drain.

I was intrigued by this. And though I knew I was not allowed to play there, I thought it wouldn't hurt just to get a bit closer to investigate. So I paddled up to the whirling water. I edged a bit closer and a bit closer. It really was very strange. What was making it circle round like that, and so quickly too? I inched nearer and craned my neck.

Then the next second it was like something under the surface reached out and snatched my legs. My feet shot out from under me and I was dragged into that whirling water. Round and round I went, arms scraping on the bottom; head under and up again, legs kicking. I just couldn't seem to stand up. Every time I got my legs down, they were torn away again. I was screaming and spluttering, going under, then pulling my head out, gasping desperately for air.

And then suddenly I looked up and saw someone coming over the top of the bridge. It was Martin Glennon, who lived just outside the village. He was a bit older than me and went everywhere on his bike and now there he was, heading home from school. I must have been making quite a noise because he suddenly looked over the bridge, dropped his bike, jumped over the fence and ran down the bank into the water. Somehow he managed to grab a wildly flailing arm and drag me out.

I stood there on the bank, water streaming off me, gasping and coughing. Martin had probably saved my life but I wasn't really aware of it. Now I knew why you weren't supposed to go under the bridge - but I still didn't understand what was wrong with that water.

'You'd better get home Peg,' said Martin staring at my dripping clothes. 'What's your Mammy going to say?'

What indeed? I daren't confess to Mammy, she'd be furious.

'I slipped and fell in.' I muttered when I finally squelched indoors. I'm not sure she believed me but I was sent upstairs to get out of my wet clothes and wrapped in a warm towel. And from then on, I lost all desire to investigate the swirling water up-stream.

Yet other odd things happened that could be unsettling. One night Mammy asked me to go up to the little shop for a loaf of bread. It was about eight thirty in the evening but in those days shops didn't have set opening hours like they do now.

At the end of the terrace there was a tiny little cottage which the elderly couple who lived there had turned into a shop. If they happened to be closed, you just knocked on the door, told them what you wanted and they'd go and get it for you.

So this particular evening I was skipping along to buy the bread when suddenly I saw a big light in the sky. It got brighter and brighter, bigger and bigger and as I stood there open mouthed, a great flaming ball of fire shot across the sky and came down in the field opposite. I saw it land in the grass.

Terrified I turned right round and raced home.

'Have you got the bread?' asked Mammy as I rushed in.

No!' I cried, my face wet with frightened tears, 'The sky's on fire!'

'What on earth are you talking about?' asked Mammy.

'A big ball of fire came out of the sky! It came down in the field!' I said.

'Oh for goodness sake Peg,' said Mammy. She went over to the window and looked out. 'I can't see any fire. The field's not on fire and the sky is not on fire! Whatever will you say next? And what are we to do for breakfast in the morning without a loaf of bread?'

Was it a meteorite I wonder now? Or some sort of ball of lightening? Or some mysterious light that was invisible to everyone else? Who knows, but it certainly frightened the life out of me.

As I grew older it was easier to keep quiet about the things I saw that other people didn't. In fact I hardly gave it a thought any more. It was completely normal to me to say nothing. Yet there were times when it wasn't so much what I saw as I somehow knew just what to do.

One day I went with some friends to the little cinema in Freshford. We went up there on our bikes, just a few girls and boys to the little hall with the bench seats where you could watch an old film for sixpence and we'd eat sticky penny chews and fizzy bags - sherbet with lolly-pops and enjoy ourselves. I particularly loved it when they showed a film about King

Arthur and those gallant Knights of the Round Table - how lovely it must have been to live in those days I often thought.

My Aunt Sarah used to live near the cinema and this particular day on the way home I was suddenly seized with the idea that I wanted to call in and see her. 'I think I'll visit my Aunt Sarah while we're here.' I said to my friend as we pedalled away.

So we cycled up to the terrace where Aunt Sarah lived and knocked on the door. There was no answer but somehow I felt she was at home. Nobody bothered locking their doors in those days so I lifted the latch and went in and there was Aunt Sarah on the floor on her hands and knees - apparently unable to stand or even to speak to us.

'What's wrong?!' cried my friend in alarm.

I stared at Aunt Sarah anxiously. She was looking up at me with desperate eyes and shakily, she lifted her arm and pointed towards the fire. Instantly I realised she was trying to show us the kettle. 'She wants steam!' I thought. So I quickly filled the kettle and put it on the fire. After a few minutes the steam came pouring out and Aunt Sarah began to recover. It turned out she'd had an asthma attack.

After sitting in the steam for a while and drinking a cup of sweet tea, Aunt Sarah was her old self again and I was so pleased we'd dropped in to say hello.

But I was growing up. I began to notice boys and also my own appearance - or at least my clothes - in particular my footwear. I had lace up boots - ugly, brown ones. To be fair most of us did. But Mammy was always saying: 'Go up to Paddy's and get him to put a metal stud on your shoe to stop it from wearing down.'

Paddy Kelly was the blacksmith. He and his wife Sally lived by the forge in a tiny cottage with walls so black and dark with smoke it was like a cave. Sometimes they papered over the soot with newspaper and for a brief while the cottage would be transformed - so light and bright and covered in interesting things to read. But the newspaper soon darkened, the background turned as black as the print and it was back to the cave again.

Paddy would patiently hammer little metal studs into the heels of my boots when requested, but I hated them. When you walked they made you clip-clop like a horse which was really embarrassing if there was a boy at school I liked. I'd walk quietly into Paddy's like a proper person and clip-clop out like a cart horse - so ashamed. But it was the only way to make the shoes last.

When I was about twelve years old I started work. I was still at school but after lessons ended, I'd go to Mr Downey, the butchers' house and clean for his wife and help look after their twins.

For some reason Mrs Downey didn't take to me, though I was fascinated by her. She had dark curly hair and was always very smartly dressed. Her shoes in particular were fascinating. Dainty little kitten-heeled things in a whole range of colours. I couldn't help staring at them. After my big clumpy old boots, they were a revelation.

Mrs Downey always found plenty of work for me. I scrubbed the floors and washed the windows, scoured the oven or tackled a pile of dirty dishes. But I was so proud to be getting paid. I earned £2 a week which of course went straight to Mammy and was badly needed.

Better still, Mrs Downey's parents sometimes came over to visit and when they saw me working away they often gave me a whole half a crown for myself. I'd thank them of course, then take the big silver coin and hide it away at home, saying nothing to anyone until the next time I saw that certain look come over Mammy's face. I knew that look well by now. It was the look of hardship - the look that meant she had no money to put food on the table and a whole host of hungry mouths to feed - because my little brothers and sisters still kept on arriving and the house was getting quite crowded.

'Don't worry Mammy,' I'd say, now so grown-up with secret coins of my own, 'I have some money. I'll buy some bread.'

And I'd hurry off to the little shop down the terrace, feeling so very proud, to fetch a crusty loaf for the family.

The work didn't bother me and as well as Mrs Downey's kind parents there were other compensations. Sometimes Mrs Downey went out, leaving me to mind the children and once, when I'd got them settled, quietly colouring by the fire, I slipped upstairs to have a look at Mrs Downey's latest new shoes.

I'd caught a glimpse of them a few days before, but now here they were in her bedroom - a wonder to behold. Red! Red shoes with a white square on the toe and neat little heels. The prettiest things I'd ever seen.

I couldn't help it. I tugged off my ugly old boots and slipped my feet into Mrs Downey's red shoes. Fortunately I was small and my feet fitted easily into the shoes with room to spare. So, quietly as I could, I tiptoed up and down, staring in amazement at my feet, now so dainty and smart. They made me look like a princess, I reckoned. I loved them.

Then a door creaked downstairs, so I quickly jumped out of the shoes, put them back beside the bed, jammed my feet into the boots and scrambled out onto the landing, laces flapping any old how. I think I got away with it!

The pavement curved round a slope above the Downey's house and one evening when I'd been working there for a few years I was on my hands and knees scrubbing the floor when a shadow fell across the bucket. I looked up through the window high in the wall and saw Daddy walking by with his little suitcase. He was home again and I hadn't met the train!

Then there was a knock on the door. Mrs Downey went to answer it and I heard Daddy's voice say: 'Can you get my daughter out here please?'

'She's not finished yet,' said Mrs Downey. 'She is now,' said Daddy, 'Get her out here.'

Mrs Downey daren't argue. I dropped the scrubbing brush back into the bucket, my working day finished early and minutes later I was skipping home beside Daddy, so delighted to see him again.

Somehow I don't think Mrs Downey took to Daddy either.

∞CHAPTER 5∞

ENGLAND SEEMED A VERY LONG WAY AWAY.....

Wow! I could hardly believe my eyes. There I was, sitting high up on the deck of this gigantic boat, with seagulls screaming round my head, my hair streaming out behind me, a wild wind blowing in my face, covering my lips with tangy salt and whipping stinging curls across my cheeks. All around, this gushing, plunging, endlessly moving, green-grey water. I'd never seen anything so exciting.

Delighted, I ripped open the packet of cheese sandwiches Mammy had made me for the journey, tore them into chunks and held them out to the gulls. They were so tame – or were they just bold!? Quite unlike the shy little birds we had at home. They swooped down, all curving yellow beaks and scaly feet, grabbed the bread out of my hands and powered away on strong, grey-fringed wings only to circle round and swoop back for more. Fearless they were. Quite fearless. They stared at me with their fierce little eyes and I stared right back, enchanted. I was so disappointed when I came to the end of Mammy's sandwiches.

I'd never even seen the sea before, not once. But now, here I was right on it – sailing away from Ireland, off to a new life in the foreign land that was England. Such an adventure!

I was sixteen years old and in Ballyragget, when a girl got to the age of 16 it was time to go out into the world and help support the family. There weren't too many jobs in the village but across the sea in England it seemed, there was endless demand for strong, young Irish girls who were polite and modestly reared and knew how to clean and help out with children.

Special agencies had sprung up to connect the English employers with us starry-eyed young school leavers and by the time my turn came along, the well- trodden route was completely familiar to parents in Ballyragget. They were sad to see their daughters leave of course but families were large, houses small and it was hard to feed all those children. A daughter who secured a good, live-in cleaning job across the water would be well fed, send money home and also free up space in the bed for her growing sisters.

In 1960, as my sixteenth birthday crept closer, Mammy had a word with Bridie Blanch who lived up the lane. Bridie was an educated woman and she was the local letter writer. For two shillings she'd write and send a letter of application to Miss Brophy's agency in England – which had found cleaning jobs for many a Ballyragget girl.

'Right Peg', Mammy said when she came back from Bridie's, 'Bridie says you need to get a reference. Go and ask Mrs Downey, you've been working for her for long enough.'

But as I suspected, Mrs Downey never did take to me. Perhaps, despite her irritation at my ways, she was also annoyed I wanted to leave. Perhaps she'd never forgiven daddy for taking me away from my work that day or maybe she'd found out about the shoes? Who knows? At any rate, she wasn't welcoming and her expression got colder and colder as I stammered out my request for a few lines of recommendation to send to England.

'Peg turn around,' she said icily when I'd finished, 'Look at that gate there. I wouldn't give you a reference to go as far as that gate.'

For a second I couldn't take in what she meant. Then it dawned on me. She was saying no. After all those hours scrubbing her floors and minding her children, she didn't think I'd earned a reference.

Crushed, I went home to Mammy. Mammy was furious of course but she wasn't going to let a rebuff from the likes of Mrs Downey stand in the way of me and my new career. She went back to Bridie and somehow they got round the problem. Perhaps they persuaded some other neighbour to testify to my honest and hard-working nature, I don't know. But whatever they did, it worked. Soon afterwards we got a letter saying I'd been accepted by Miss Brophy's agency and shortly afterwards the news came that an ideal cleaning job had been found for me at a Catholic boarding school in a village called Mill Hill, just outside London.

England seemed a very long way away and I'd travelled absolutely nowhere in my 16 years, yet I felt excited more than nervous. Mammy found me a little square suitcase for my few possessions. Bridie wrote a note for me to hand to the Station Master when I got to Dublin, asking him to put me on the boat train and we picked a bunch of green shamrocks to pin to my coat, so that the agency lady would recognise me when I stepped off the boat at Holyhead.

Then we walked to Ballyragget station and Mammy put me on the train to Dublin with my suitcase and my sandwiches. Her heart must have been breaking but there was no way she was going to let me see her cry.

'Now don't lose that note Peg,' she said briskly as the train puffed up to the platform, 'and don't forget to write.' And with a quick hug she pushed me into a carriage, the door slammed, the guard blew his whistle and suddenly we were pulling away down the line towards the big city. I felt just like Daddy, waving out the window as Mammy and my brothers and sisters stood on the platform waving back and Ballyragget slowly slid away until every last cottage had disappeared, the train gathered speed and all I could see was the green Irish countryside rushing past.

For a while there was a strange heaviness in my chest that I couldn't quite understand, but then the excitement began to bubble up again and soon I was craning out the window, eager for the first glimpse of the city.

Dublin station was a revelation; so big and bustling and smoky, with platforms all over the place and huge engines coming and going with ear-splitting roars and clouds of steam. In a daze I stumbled along, clutching my little case until I spotted an impressive figure in a smart uniform, carrying a lamp.

Excuse me sir,' I said nervously, 'Can you help?' and I showed him my note. He read it silently.

'Right you are then,' he said, 'Wait there a minute.' He went off, checked the times and returned a few minutes later to take me to the boat train.

'Now the train goes right to the boat at Dun Laoghaire,' he said, 'so just stay there and you won't get lost.'

Sure enough the train took me all the way to my first magical encounter with the sea. Everything astonished me. The huge boat, the crowds of people, the extraordinary endless waves, yet I didn't feel frightened. Somehow I just took it for granted that people would look out for me – and they did.

At Holyhead, we all had to file off the boat and down to the quayside. My boots touched English soil for the first time. I stood blankly on the dock hanging onto my suitcase while the crowds streamed round me – unsure what to do or where to go. For a moment I was a bit lost, a bit like Alice in Wonderland, but then a woman stepped forward, peered at the battered shamrocks pinned to my coat and said: 'Are you Peg? I'm from Miss Brophy's agency and I'm taking you to St Vincent's in Mill Hill. You'll like it there. There are a lot of Irish girls already working there. You'll soon make friends.'

So off we went again on more trains; from Holyhead to London and then on to the prosperous little village of Mill Hill. My eyes felt like they were falling out of my head the whole time. England was so big and so busy and the posh English voices echoed round, so loud and so grand - and the English girls! I couldn't get over those smart English girls! Everywhere I looked, there were these exotic creatures with short, straight skirts that showed their knees for everyone to see and their high heeled shoes. Click, clack, click, they went when they walked, so elegant and refined, displaying their knees all glamorously encased in tan stockings, without a blush. 'Brazen' the nuns would have called them. Quite shockingly brazen.

Yet I marvelled at them. The way they click-clacked along the pavements, heads held high, so brisk and confident and fashionable. Beside these film star creatures, in my long Irish skirts and clumpy boots I felt hopelessly unsophisticated. And it wasn't just my clothes. Ballyragget ways ran through me like the letters through a stick of rock. Every time the wind blew, my hands flew instantly to my billowing skirts, fighting them down and frantically clamping them round my knees. I just couldn't help it. How those English girls would have smiled to see me.

Fortunately at St Vincent's there were plenty of Irish girls just like me. St Vincent's was a big, sprawling, much altered brick building next door to the convent, which occupied a house built in the 17th century. There were lovely grounds with big trees, a pretty chapel and a long driveway that led out to the main road.

Quite a few boys and girls seemed to board there but we didn't have much time to talk to them. We kept busy cleaning and polishing. My special friend was a girl called Maria from Galway and one afternoon, during a break we decided to go out and investigate Mill Hill.

We walked up the long drive to the gate and as we got there, we noticed two boys on the other side of the road.

One of them in particular was gorgeous. Slim and dark haired with this little quiff just like Elvis Presley – and I loved Elvis. I knew England was good but I didn't realise it was THIS good, I thought to myself. 'Oh look, they're smiling at us,' said Maria. 'Don't look! Don't look!' I shushed her, quickly turning my head away from the boys and pretending a sudden interest in a very attractive bush beside the gate.

'Why not?' asked Maria, puzzled. 'They'll think we like them.' I sighed. 'Well we do!' said Maria even more puzzled. 'Yes, but don't let them know that yet!'

But all the time I was looking at them out of the corner of my eye. They were smiling our way and definitely interested but I was determined not to let them guess that we were interested too. So Maria and I took a stroll up the street and back again, proud as two princesses, heads held high, deep in conversation and apparently completely unaware of the presence of two male admirers.

After that, Maria and I somehow found ourselves free for a stroll at the same time every afternoon – and strangely enough, so did the two boys. They were probably on their way home from school because they were clearly a similar age to us.

Little by little we explored the sights of Mill Hill – the village pond, the few tiny shops, the grand houses now turned into schools and other institutions and the pretty old cottages – but better than any of that - we were now on smiling terms with the two boys!

One day I couldn't help noticing that my Elvis look-alike had appeared with a big bandage on his hand.

'Oh look!' whispered soft hearted Maria, 'He's hurt himself. 'Don't take any notice,' I whispered back, 'I expect he's just pretending to attract attention.' Where I got these ideas from I can't imagine –maybe it was all those years with Uncle Neddy and his practical jokes.

But after a week, Elvis was still wearing the bandage and I had to admit that if he was just out for attention and sympathy, he was carrying the joke a bit far.

In the end I couldn't help myself. 'What happened to your hand?' I asked.

Instantly the boy was at my side. 'I help out in the butchers after school,' he said eagerly, his greeny hazel eyes sparkling and looking more Elvis like than ever, 'Caught my hand when I was chopping meat.'

And that was it. The ice was broken. Turned out his name was Tony, he lived in the village and he was sixteen just like me. He could never have guessed from my cool, nonchalant manner but I was already in love with him. It had been love at first sight – from that very first moment by the gate I'd known he was the one for me. I wasn't going to tell him that of course – not for ages, but for now, I had my first boyfriend. England just got better and better.

∞CHAPTER 6∞

DADDY'S IDEA OF AN EMERGENCY WASN'T THE SAME AS MINE!

Although we didn't realise it then, as 1960 moved into 1961, the decade, that was soon to become famous ever since as the 'Swinging Sixties' was just beginning to rev into life. Unwittingly, Tony and I were just a few miles from the heart of the action in London – soon to make its mark as the most fashionable city in the world. It was a wonderful time to be young and in love.

Not that Tony and I knew anything then of newly trendy addresses like Carnaby Street and the Kings Road, Chelsea, but even in the quiet village atmosphere of Mill Hill, news filtered through of a young dress designer called Mary Quant, who was destined to change the face of fashion, and a pop group known as the Beatles.

Tony was very taken with the Beatles when their records started to climb the charts, he even bought a single called 'I Wanna Hold Your Hand', but somehow they left me cold. Their fresh faces and odd, pudding-basin hair-cuts didn't impress me at all. My heart belonged to Elvis. He was gorgeous of course and nothing could compare to that incredible raw rock 'n' roll voice, beautiful face and dark quiff and he knew how to shake, as far as I was concerned. What was there not to like?!

At first, my dates with Tony consisted mainly of going out for walks through the village and around the pond. Then after a while, he took me home to meet his parents, Rose and Charlie and his sisters and brother at their little house nearby. They were a lovely family – Rose so lively and vivacious and Charlie quieter and more thoughtful. I discovered later that Charlie had served with the Desert Rats during the war and ended up being seriously wounded. He was paralysed for a while. He never talked about it, but after surgery and months of treatment he was able to walk again but he was left with a limp and he was often in pain, though he never once complained.

Rose and Charlie were always kind to me though, and I loved to be back in a hectic, family atmosphere. I wasn't consciously homesick, as I was too busy being in love, but I missed Mammy and my brothers and sisters and our noisy, crowded house in Ballyragget. Visiting the Weber's made up a little for not having my own family close by.

Much as I would have loved to talk to Mammy, Mammy, like most mothers in the terrace, didn't have the luxury of a phone, so we could only keep in touch by post, or on the very odd occasion, she would have to walk up to the phone box on the square. The mail was very slow though and neither of us was a good letter writer. Fortunately, in emergencies I could phone Daddy at his barracks in Kildare where the sentry had a phone on the gate. Daddy had written the number down for me and I kept it safe.

The trouble was Daddy's idea of an emergency and mine were on a completely different scale. Also, I had no idea of what a barracks was like, either the layout or the daily routine. It never occurred to me when I felt a powerful urge to talk to Daddy and slipped out to the public phone box with my pennies, that the sentry would have to send someone to go and find him and bring him all the way down to the phone, or even get him out of bed and drag him out to the gate to take my call.

One night I just wanted to say: 'Daddy I've met this lovely boy...'

Another night, distraught after a tiff with Tony, I called Daddy at 01:00 am.

There was a very long wait as a soldier was despatched to rouse Daddy from sleep. Then finally his familiar voice came over the line. 'Jesus, Peg! Why are you phoning?'

'Oh Daddy!' I wailed, completely failing to notice his anxious tone, 'Tony won't talk to me! We've had an argument.'

Daddy wasn't best pleased by this latest emergency. He told me to go back to bed and get some sleep, it probably wasn't as serious as I thought and I could make it up with Tony the next day - which of course is exactly what happened. Daddy was right again!

As time passed, Tony and our circle of friends began to explore further afield. One boy acquired a car – an almost unheard of extravagance then. It was a big blue convertible, all bright and shiny with lavish splashes of chrome and a sleek black hood that you could fold down when it wasn't raining.

This was the era when coffee bars were cool and we'd drive out to the latest 'in' place, which happened to be a few miles away in Watford, to drink frothy coffee out of tall see-through glass mugs, play music on the juke box and jive. Tony and I taught ourselves to jive and we loved it. We even reckoned we got pretty good at it and took every opportunity to show off when we could!

By this time I was able to put a small deposit down until I could pay for an item or two of this amazing new London fashion coming through. I bought high heel shoes, real nylon stockings and the dresses with big, full skirts and loads of underskirts that were fashionable then. It was difficult to sit down in them but we didn't care. I even acquired an immensely trendy coat by Mary Quant herself – it was an eye catching and knee length with unusual navy and white candy stripes. I felt very stylish in my new coat. What a shame I didn't hang onto it!

When we went out for the evening we'd pack ourselves in the car, four in the back, three in the front, us girls squeezed together on the back seat with all our petticoats round our ears. Then we'd tear through the streets towards a coffee bar or the Irish centre of Cricklewood and the Galtymore Ballroom, so famous with the Irish community that when it finally closed in 2008, it made the papers back home in Ireland.

The other exciting thing about having access to a car was the new road they were building near Mill Hill – an extension to the incredibly exciting M1 – England's very first, full length motorway which had opened in 1959 - just a year before I arrived in the country. In those days there was no central reservation, no speed limit and very few drivers had seen anything like it. There weren't many cars around then, but those that found their way to the M1 tended to treat it like a race track.

And now it was coming within a whisker of Mill Hill. We went exploring in the blue convertible and found a place where the new road, still under construction, was separated from a neighbouring suburban street by nothing more than a row of cones.

We got out of the car and gazed awestruck, up the vast empty ribbon of concrete. It stretched away north, as far as the eye could see, grey, dead straight, flat enough to drive on and completely deserted.

'Hey!' cried Tony, 'Let's see where it goes!'

So we moved the cones, jumped back in the car and set out up the new motorway. Maybe it was a bit bumpy, maybe the proper surface hadn't yet been laid, I can't remember, but the blue convertible bounced along the dusty track and got us through.

After a while we came to a place where the extension joined the existing M1, so we zipped across, pulled into the light traffic and carried on up the motorway to the modern new town of Hemel Hempstead, itself still partly under construction.

We couldn't believe how fast we'd got there. It seemed amazing to us to be able to reach another town in the heart of the countryside so quickly. Of course after that, we couldn't wait to do it again.

Soon it became a regular outing. At night, when no one was around, we'd drive up to the new road, move the cones, put the hood down on the convertible and race up the deserted motorway to Hemel Hempstead, as fast as we could go, the wind tearing through our hair and trying to drag our petticoats over our heads.

When we arrived, we went to the cinema or the ten-pin bowling alley, (another new craze) and afterwards we'd get back in the car and go racing home again, not forgetting to restore the cones before we slipped back onto the quiet residential roads.

There was never any doubt in my mind that Tony was the boy for me and as the months slipped into years, we just took it for granted that one day we'd get married. There was no formal proposal and I wasn't bothered about an engagement ring, but I did want to take Tony home to meet my family.

He'd left school by then and was working in a butcher's shop, so we saved our wages until we had enough cash to pay for a trip to Ballyragget.

It was a great success. It was wonderful to see Mammy and Daddy again and my brothers and sisters, all grown so much taller. They loved Tony of course, as I'd known they would, particularly Michael, a cheeky little lad with a singing voice like an angel when I'd left, now a big boy of 12 with a newly discovered talent for hurling. He hung around Tony whenever he could and offered to show him how to play our traditional Irish sport.

As far as I was concerned I couldn't wait for the Saturday night dancing in the pub. I was dying to show off my jiving and I felt certain that Ballyragget had never seen anything like Tony and I in action! Sure enough, afterwards, the village girls crowded round, fascinated as much by my clothes as my dancing skills. 'God, you've got real high heel shoes!' 'Look at your skirt! All those petticoats!' And 'Oh....proper stockings!' London was clearly the height of sophistication in their eyes and I must admit, I basked in their admiration. Or, at least I did until they turned their attention to Tony.

'And your fiancé. Isn't he handsome!' they cooed.

That brought me down to earth. 'You keep your eyes to yourself!' I joked and went and linked my arm through Tony's to make quite sure they got the message.

The music and dancing went on and on and it was a great night but then suddenly at about 10.30, everything went quiet. The music paused, and looking round to see what had happened I noticed the priest had come in. Then to my horror, I realised that he was walking straight towards me.

'I believe you're one of the Nealis girls,' he said abruptly.

'Yes.' I said, blushing but puzzled.

'I am also led to believe you've got your future husband with you,' he looked piercingly at Tony, 'and he's not Catholic.'

Embarrassment began to give way to anger. 'So?' I said.

'Tell him to come up to the house tomorrow.'

'What for?' I asked, dimly aware of a little murmur of shock, ripple round the curious audience that was gathering. You didn't question the priest!

'I want him to become Catholic.'

Tony was blushing now and looking very embarrassed. I moved closer to him.

'No,' I said. 'No?' The priest looked outraged. You didn't say no to the priest either. 'He has to be Catholic or your marriage won't be recognised in the eyes of the Church.'

'I will be married in the eyes of God.' I said defiantly.

The priest was turning rather red but he kept his voice quiet and restrained.

'Well d'you mind me asking where you intend to get married?' he said, clearly thinking he'd played his trump card.

I hadn't given it much thought until that point but before I knew it, the words just popped out of my mouth.

'In a registry office.' I said, knowing full well that this was the most annoying, offensive thing I could say.

'Well you will not be welcome in Ireland anymore.' He said and swept angrily away.

'D'you hear that babe?' I said to Tony, who was looking like he wanted the ground to swallow him up. I raised my voice to make sure everyone could hear. 'That's good because if it doesn't work out we won't need to divorce as we won't be married!'

The music started up again and we swung into a jig as if we didn't have a care in the world, but inside I was angry and upset. How could that horrible priest have spoiled my lovely homecoming with Tony?

But it wasn't completely spoiled. I tried to put the incident out of my mind and we still had plenty of fun at home. One day Mammy and Uncle Neddy decided to play a joke on Tony. They were still working in the fields, picking potatoes and tending to the other crops. 'Don't say anything to Tony,' Mammy whispered to me, 'we're going to play a little trick.'

'Tony,' she went on loudly, 'Neddy and me are off to thin the beet. Would you like to come?'

But to Tony's English ears it sounded as if she'd said 'tin the beet'. And he assumed they were going to some canning factory that he'd not so far seen. He was desperate to make a good impression on my family, so he agreed eagerly and went to get dressed in his best, light grey Italian suit, thin leather shoes and his hair smartly slicked back – all ready for a day in town at the factory.

Later that afternoon he got home looking exhausted and Mammy and Uncle Neddy were laughing hysterically. Fortunately Tony saw the funny side too.

'I couldn't see a factory anywhere Peg,' he told me afterwards, 'All the way up the lane I was looking for one but all I could see was fields. Then they turned into this muddy field and gave me a pile of sacks to put on my knees. Uncle Neddy showed me how to tie them round each leg with string and we were picking beets all day.'

Thank goodness his lovely suit wasn't ruined. But he took it so well. Mammy cooked up a huge pan of potatoes and we all sat down to a hilarious meal – with Tony now well and truly one of the family, Catholic or not.

∞CHAPTER 7∞

TONY LOOKED SO HANDSOME IN HIS GREY SUIT

We were perfectly happy, Tony and I. We were in love, our families approved and one day we knew, we'd get married. I wasn't bothered by conventional ideas like having an engagement ring. Tony was all I needed, not a ring on my finger, so why waste money we didn't have on a useless piece of jewellery? But we weren't planning ahead, weren't really thinking of anything except how much we enjoyed being together and having fun.

And perhaps we'd have gone on like that, quite content, for years. But then early in 1965 fate took a hand and I discovered I was pregnant.

'Don't worry babe!' said Tony cheerfully when I told him, 'We'll get married.'

We were both only 20 at the time but back then people tended to marry and raise families at an earlier age than they do today, so it didn't seem too surprising. And though I hadn't planned to become a mum so soon, I was used to babies and looking after children so the prospect wasn't too alarming.

Back in the Ireland of the early sixties though, having a baby out of wedlock would have been shameful. I can just imagine the look on the priest's face if I'd come home with an infant in my arms and no ring on my finger. Not that I cared what he thought of course, but it was a different world. I still recalled with a shudder those whispered stories of unmarried girls being cared for by the nuns in convents for weeks on end and then emerging, sad and pale without their babies. In most cases, they never saw their little ones again.

But that wasn't going to happen to me. Tony booked us up at our local registry office in Hendon, (just as I'd predicted so thoughtlessly all those months ago to the priest in Ballyragget). His parents secured the village hall for a reception and invitations were sent out to friends and relatives.

I went to Watford and bought a pretty pale blue coat and a little blue hat to match, and then together we found a jeweller and chose a simple gold wedding band. We were all set.

Finally on a bright, blustery day on March 27th we were married. Tony looked handsome in a grey suit and I brightened up my blue coat with a flower in the button hole. The little ceremony was short. It seemed to race by in a blur and within minutes, or at least it felt like only minutes, we were walking out of Hendon Registry office, hand in hand as the new Mr and Mrs Weber. I was so proud. It really was the happiest day of my life. I couldn't think of any better future than being Tony's wife.

Sadly my family couldn't make the journey from Ireland to be with us but all of Tony's relatives and most of our friends were there. It wasn't a lavish affair by today's standards. Everyone banded together to help but that meant more to us than any fancy do with starched table cloths and waiters. Aunties and Uncles staggered in with big trays of food they'd made at home – sandwiches and sausage rolls and pork pies - and Tony's Uncle Ron who worked for Vauxhall making cars brought a keg of beer. Our friends supplied a record player and a stack of '60's records and soon the village inn (now known as The Adam & Eve Gastro Pub) was rocking with a fine old party!

Between the jiving and the laughter my eyes kept being drawn back to the beautiful gold band gleaming on my finger. I couldn't stop looking at it. I was Mrs Weber. 'Mrs Weber'.

From now on I had a new name. I felt so happy I couldn't have had a better day if we'd got married at the Ritz.

After the wedding we went back to Tony's parents' house where we were going to live until we found our own place. A honeymoon was out of the question. There was no money to spare for holidays. From now on we would have to be careful with every penny.

But Tony had ideas. He'd seen an advert for a butcher's assistant some distance away in Suffolk and the pay was better than in his current job in Mill Hill. He was invited along for an interview and over the phone the butcher sounded so enthusiastic about Tony's chances we felt there was a real prospect of us settling down with our new family in Suffolk.

The only problem was, in those days Suffolk was much more remote and rural than it is now and getting there from Mill Hill by public transport would probably take hours and be extremely difficult. Tony was very close to his parents and he was worried we'd hardly ever see them if we moved away.

'You know what Peg – we'll have to get a car.' he said. He'd already passed his driving test in case he ever needed to drive the butcher's van so he started looking out for an old banger of a car. A few days later he came home with a battered old green Vauxhall he'd found for £37 – which happened to be the bulk of our savings.

It wasn't exactly a limousine and there was quite a bit of rust but it worked. I was thrilled. There were still thousands of families without access to any kind of car so we felt very lucky and privileged. After a few test drives to reassure ourselves it would stand up to a long journey, off we went to Suffolk in our lucky green Vauxhall. After all, if Tony got the job, we were going to live down there so it would be good to take a look at the area.

Suffolk turned out to be a pretty place; green and gently rolling with little thatched cottages painted in rainbow shades of cream, pink and white, that really did look like something you saw on a chocolate box. It was very rural, which of course I was used to, so living there would be no problem at all I thought.

Unfortunately there was some sort of mix up with the interview though. When Tony went to see the butcher, he came back with the news that the interview had to be put off for a couple of days. Trouble was, the roads were nothing like they are today and it had taken us hours to get here. It was too far to drive back and return again.

'We'll just have to sleep in the car babe.' said Tony.

We were young and I'd not exactly been brought up in the lap of luxury, so this idea didn't bother me too much but Tony wasn't happy about it. I was pregnant after all and we didn't have blankets or pillows. He was worried I'd catch a cold. We strolled up and down the village street deciding what to do for the best and out of habit, paused to read the little 'for sale' ads on postcards in a shop window.

One of them leapt out immediately. 'Room to rent' it said.

'I wonder if it's still free?' said Tony, 'Maybe if it's not taken yet they'd let us stay overnight....'

'But we haven't got any money,' I reminded him.

'Can't hurt to ask.' said Tony.

Next thing I knew he was striding down to the red telephone box across the road and dialling the number.

'So sorry to bother you...it's about the room...' I heard him say, 'but my wife's pregnant and we've got nowhere to stay tonight... thing is though, we can't pay....'

Honestly, I was thinking. What a nerve she'll think he's got – asking to stay for free. She's bound to send him packing. But the next second, to my complete amazement, Tony was thanking her and jotting down an address.

A few minutes later he emerged from the phone box beaming all over his face. 'She said it was alright!' said Tony in delight, 'She said bring your wife over. She can't sleep in the car and the place is just round the corner.'

We followed the directions and soon found ourselves outside a beautiful cream painted thatched cottage. The room for rent was in a small annexe attached to the main building and overlooking the garden. What's more, by the time we arrived, the woman who was a widow and lived alone, had made us a pot of tea and a pile of sandwiches – despite knowing we had no money. What a lovely lady.

We were very comfortable in our cosy room. There was just one strange incident. All my life, I'd been the one who saw odd things; inexplicable lights and people who seemed to be invisible to others, but that night it was Tony's turn to have a psychic experience.

I was so tired after the journey I sank gratefully into the soft bed and fell straight into a deep sleep. Tony though, woke up in the early hours and saw a ghost.

'I'm not kidding Peg, I really did.' he told me the next morning. 'I woke up and there was a man standing at the foot of the bed. He was tall and he was wearing a long fur coat and he had a little cap on his head.'

'What did he do?' I asked, fascinated.

'Nothing. He just stood there looking at us and then he just faded away.'

I was the last person to say people were imagining things, so naturally I believed him completely, but it was clear that the man, whoever he was, meant us no harm so I wasn't worried. The room had a happy atmosphere and we felt quite content there. In fact it suited us all so well that the kind lady invited us to stay on for another few days.

Tony went for his interview and got the job but it turned out they didn't need the new assistant to start for a few months yet. This was probably just as well as it would give us time to sort out somewhere to live.

Thanks to the kind lady in the cottage we were able to tour the area and get to know it a little ahead of our move. Then on our last day, the lady invited us for Sunday lunch in the main cottage. We went across and were shown into a pretty dining room overlooking the garden. But Tony's eyes were drawn straight to a photograph on the mantel piece. It showed a tall man in a long fur coat, almost to his ankles with a little cap on his head.

Tony had gone white. 'Who's that in the photo?' he asked the woman.

'Oh that's my late husband,' she said, 'He was an opera singer. That's him on stage at Covent Garden. He often wore that costume.'

When she went out to fetch the roast, Tony rushed over to look at the picture more closely.

'That's him!' he said, 'That's the man at the foot of the bed. The ghost.'

It made perfect sense to me. 'Well I expect he was checking us out,' I said, 'making sure his wife was safe with us.' And I reckon he approved, because that was the last Tony saw of him.

While we waited for Tony's new job to start, a friend told us about a room we could rent in Kensal Rise, North London. It was at the top of a tall Victorian house. There was just the one room with a tiny kitchenette with two gas rings and a mini sink in it, the bathroom was outside on the landing and shared by all of the lodgers. There was no central heating of course; just a little two bar electric fire, but the landlady wasn't keen on us using it.

She used to creep up the stairs from her quarters below and stop a few steps down from the landing so that she could see what sort of light was coming from under our door. If it was suspiciously orange and glowing she'd call out: 'Would you turn the fire off please!' And we'd have to reluctantly switch it off.

Despite this, Tony and I were happy there. We'd grown up seeing our parents make do and mend so it wasn't a problem for us.

Our little daughter was born on September 23rd in St Mary's hospital Paddington, weighing in at a fraction less than 7lbs with a mop of dark hair like her daddy and her daddy's determined chin. We decided to call her Teresa – in honour of Mammy's statue. It didn't occur to me at the time but maybe Mammy's favourite saint was in the back of mind. Anyway the name seemed to suit her and we thought she was absolutely gorgeous.

We took baby Teresa back to our room in Kensal Rise and made her a snug wooden crib out of a drawer from the chest. She was perfectly happy in that and the kitchen and bathroom arrangements were fine too. There was a beautiful laundrette and some shops round the corner and nearby was a pleasant park. Basically we had everything we needed.

Someone gave us an old pram and I'd spend my days wheeling Teresa out to get the washing and the shopping done, piling it all in the handy space at Teresa's feet and then we'd go on to the park for some fresh air.

What more could we want?

∞CHAPTER 8∞

I'D CATCH A BRIGHT GLOBE LIKE A SHIMMERING BUBBLE

When Teresa was just a few months old, Tony's new job at the butchers in Suffolk finally came through, and even better, we heard we were able to rent a council house in Bute Court, in the small country town of Haverhill.

After our cramped little room in the old house in Kensal Rise, it seemed spacious as a palace. Bute Court was nearly new – all pale beige bricks and big picture windows in the latest modern style, with grass verges and spindly new trees in the streets and little gardens at the back where you could hang your washing.

Everything was bright and clean and when I put Teresa out in the garden in her pram on sunny days, I knew she was filling her tiny lungs with fresh Suffolk air – not London bus fumes. It was perfect. We didn't have much money to spare but with Tony working at the butchers, there was always left-over meat that needed using up at the end of the day for him to bring home, so we never went hungry.

Our second baby, Patricia was born at home on December 2nd 1966, in such a hurry to arrive she shot into the world like a skinny little whippet, with a mass of blonde hair just like Mammy's. The girls were followed a few years later by two boys, Paul on 4th May 1969 and Phil on 4th July 1970 and Tony could not have been a more proud dad.

As far as we were concerned we had the ideal family – two of each. It was a very happy, busy time in our lives and with four small children to care for, my mind was very much occupied with down to earth, practical matters. The odd happenings of my childhood seemed to fade into the background – hardly relevant now.

I still thought of my magic lights now and then of course and occasionally, out of the corner of my eye as dusk was falling, I'd catch a bright globe, like a shimmering, transparent bubble, sliding across the ceiling or wandering across a wall. And I'd think to myself: 'Hmmm, my magic lights have got big...' But apart from that I scarcely gave them a thought. It seemed to me they were probably spirit visitors – entirely natural, nothing to worry about but nothing to get particularly excited about either - normal as the sparrows in the trees or the colourful little ladybirds that sometimes appeared on the roses.

There were odd noises too. Our house could not have been less old and spooky, yet it was often filled with peculiar creeks and bangs when the children were at school, Tony at work and there was no one home but me. Sometimes I even got the feeling that someone was watching me. It wasn't a threatening sensation though. I felt no malice from those invisible eyes – if indeed they were eyes – so I just shrugged to myself and got on with whatever I was doing. It didn't bother me at all.

Later, when we got a family camera to take snaps of the children, I noticed that occasionally, the pictures came back from the chemists where you took your film for developing in those days - with strange, circular blemishes on them. How annoying I used to think. Something must have been wrong with the film. It never occurred to me there was anything other than a mundane explanation.

The only really memorable psychic experience I can recall from my young mum days occurred at our next home, a few years later. Tony began to tire of being a butcher and took a job in sales with a craft supplies firm. We moved to the pretty village of Toddington, Bedfordshire, which was practically on top of our old favourite road - the M1 motorway. Yet despite being so close to a motorway junction, Toddington was still a proper village, surrounded by countryside and complete with green, duck pond, black and white timbered cottages and several ancient pubs.

Soon after we moved in, my brother Charlie came over from Ireland to stay with us. He'd got a job in the big car factory just one junction down the M1 from us, in Luton and our new home was ideally placed for him to get to work every day while he looked around for somewhere to live.

It was a very hot summer and one warm evening not long after Charlie arrived, the two men were home from work, the children were in bed and Tony went into the garden to pick up one of the boys' water pistols, left lying on the grass. To his surprise it still felt surprisingly heavy. He squeezed the trigger experimentally and suddenly a jet of water shot out, arched across the garden, through the open dining- room window and all over Charlie who was sitting inside.

Charlie yelled and leapt up, I went to see what was going on and the next minute the two of us were chasing round and round the dining-room table with Tony in hot pursuit, firing off streams of water at our rapidly drenching backs. We were practically crying with laughter. The weather was so warm we didn't mind a bit and a few drops of water wouldn't hurt the carpet. Giggling and squealing we raced round the room like three great big overgrown kids!

But then Tony caught up with me, and brandishing the water pistol in one hand, he grabbed me playfully by the scruff of the neck with the other. It didn't hurt at all, in fact I hardly noticed it and yet something very odd happened. The instant his fingers closed on my neck I felt myself whoosh upwards and suddenly I was looking down at the scene from somewhere near the ceiling.

I could see myself, down below by the table but now I – or rather my body - was lying on the floor and I noticed that my eyes were shut. Tony had a look of complete horror on his face. The water pistol fell from his hand and he dropped to his knees beside me and began frantically patting my face. Charlie meanwhile turned to see where we'd gone, did a double take and rushed over. He took my hand and patted it helplessly, then dashed off again and returned with a cushion which he put under my head.

Strangely, I could see their lips moving as they urged me to wake up but I couldn't seem to hear their voices. Also, thinking about it afterwards I realised I felt no strong emotion at all – I wasn't surprised, or worried or even sorry for the fright I was causing Tony and Charlie. I just watched the scene unfold with mild interest as if I was viewing a silent movie at the cinema.

Charlie hurried off to the kitchen and a few minutes later he was back with a cup of tea. I saw Tony lift my shoulders, support my head and gently put the cup to my lips. And suddenly there was another whoosh and I felt the rim of the cup against my teeth and hot, sweet liquid spilling onto my tongue and I was back. I opened my eyes and found myself looking straight into Tony's urgently anxious gaze.

'Oh Peg! Are you ok? You gave us a fright. You fainted.'

I sipped the tea. 'I don't think so,' I said, 'I saw the whole thing.'

'No babe, you didn't,' Tony assured me kindly, 'You were flat out on the floor, unconscious. Are you sure you're ok? Does anything hurt? Shall we call the doctor?'

'I'm fine.' I insisted, 'But I did. I was watching you and Charlie the whole time.' And I described how they'd patted my face and hands and got the cushion and the tea and so on, until in the end, they were as confused as I was. Back then none of us knew what to make of the odd affair, but now I know there's a name for it. I'd had what they call an 'out of body experience'.

Yet life was still too busy to give other worldly matters much attention. Particularly as in the mid-nineties another momentous event occurred that drove most other thoughts out of our heads. Tony found his biological father.

We'd known for a long time that Tony's dear dad Charlie, was not his biological father. As a teenager Tony had often puzzled as to why he had turned out different as he had darker hair with olive skin, that tanned so well, while his younger brothers and sisters were tall and slim with fair hair and paler complexions. He looked so different from them it was hard to make out much family resemblance.

Then one evening when Tony was about 14, he discovered the truth. Slipping downstairs one night to get a drink, he overheard his Mum Rose on the phone to her sister. She was talking about a man called Phil, an American GI. From the conversation it soon became clear that Rose had fallen for Phil when he was stationed at a US base in Somerset and she herself had been sent down to nearby Glastonbury to work as a Land Army girl. They'd started dating, but then Phil's unit was sent overseas to fight and he left, never knowing that Rose was pregnant.

Tony was shocked of course, but he slipped away, never admitting that he'd been listening. After all Charlie had always been a good dad to him who brought him up, and was always there for him and that's what counted. But the bombshell did at least explain why he looked so different from his brothers and sisters.

Over the years that followed Tony did try to raise the subject with his Mum now and then. She was reluctant to talk about it, but from scraps of information she let slip occasionally, he was able to work out that Rose and Charlie had known each other before the war – they'd even been engaged briefly - and when Charlie returned, badly wounded, years later, they rekindled their romance and Charlie accepted little Tony as his own son.

Phil Di Meglio, Tony's biological father was a charismatic Italian American, Rose explained. A handsome man with dark hair and olive skin just like Tony's. He was extrovert, fun-loving and exuded the kind of confidence and self-assurance that came with being ten years older than Rose. Rose was dazzled and promptly fell head over heels. Later she recalled him telling her that his family were something to do with catering, and the city Pennsylvania was mentioned. But when the war ended, she'd never heard from him again and she had no idea how to contact him.

For quite a time this information was enough for Tony. But as the years passed his curiosity grew. There were practical considerations too as he began to be frustrated by niggling health worries. He seemed to have a delicate digestive system. Various foods would unexpectedly upset him or he'd suffer uncomfortable bloating. Frequently when he went to the doctor, he was asked about his family history, if perhaps anyone else suffered similar symptoms? But of course Tony only knew about one side of his family and they were all fine. Somehow it seemed to become more and more important to him to find the missing piece of his family jigsaw for genetic health implications, to at least be aware of for our four children. Then one day he was listening to the radio and heard that there was a controversy raging about moves to give war babies the right to information about their American GI fathers. This was controversial because those children could theoretically use the information to track their fathers down - and those fathers may not want to be found.

This was the first Tony had heard about the scheme but it was just the breakthrough he'd been waiting for. He immediately wrote to the government office concerned, which in turn passed him on to the US Army Veterans Association.

Tony reckoned that with an unusual name like Di Meglio, there wouldn't be too many in Pennsylvania, so he was amazed a few weeks later when a fat envelope arrived in the post from the Army Veterans containing several closely typed sheets of ex-servicemen with the same name. He'd intended to write a diplomatically worded letter to the one or two possibilities he might receive, but this very long list was overwhelming. 'I can't write to all these.' he said, turning over page after page in despair. Actually, knowing Tony, I think he would have done. Not all at once, but so determined was he to track down his dad, that I reckon bit by bit he would have worked his way from the top of the list to the bottom, sending off a few letters at a time until he got the answer he was hoping for.

But in the end he didn't need to. He had to start somewhere so one night he picked up the pages again and stared at them very hard. Then he ran his finger down the columns until it came to a stop against one particular P. Di Meglio.

'I've got a feeling about this one.' he said.

It looked no different to any of the other P. Di Meglios to us but I've always believed you should go with your instincts and that's what Tony did. He wrote a vague letter to the ex-serviceman saying that a war commemoration was being planned in England and there were a number of people who had fond memories of a Phil Di Meglio, stationed near Glastonbury in the 1940s and would love to hear news of him.

To our surprise, not long afterwards Tony received a letter from Phil enclosing a 1940's photograph of himself in his army uniform and a telephone number. There was no doubt this was the man we were looking for. He even resembled Tony with his friendly smile and dark hair. Incredibly his hand writing could have been Tony's too! It was uncanny!

Tony spent a lot of time staring at that phone number. Then that night, he poured himself a very large whiskey and took it with him to the phone. His hands were shaking so much he could hardly dial the number, but he had to find out the truth. Phil answered and Tony took a deep breath and ploughed right in. He introduced himself and established that Phil had indeed known a girl called Rose near Glastonbury all those years ago. 'Well Phil, I must tell you that I'm your son.' said Tony.

There was a gasp, then a long silence and then a strange sound that after a while Tony realised was the sound of crying. 'My God. My God - it's my son!' said Phil when he could finally speak. And Tony found he had tears in his own eyes too.

But once the shock wore off they couldn't stop talking. Tony told Phil that as well as a son, he had a daughter in law and four lovely grandchildren. Also Rose was still alive and well too. In turn, Phil told Tony that when he'd returned from fighting in Europe, Rose had left Glastonbury. Determined to find her, he'd gone to the home address in London she'd given him but the house had been bombed and no one could tell him where the family had gone. With no clues to follow and no idea even if Rose would still be interested in him, Phil returned to the USA never knowing that Rose had been carrying his child. Eventually he married a Polish girl called Helen and they'd had a son of their own, but no grandchildren.

Father and son chatted away for hours that night and, as we discovered afterwards, when the call finally ended, old Phil went dancing out into his back garden shouting: 'I've got grandkids! I've got grandkids!' He was over the moon.

After that, there were many more phone calls and Tony even arranged for Rose and Phil to have a private talk. We didn't eavesdrop, but from the length of time they were chatting and the bursts of laughter that kept coming from Rose, we gathered they still got on like a house on fire. When she finally put the phone down she was lit up like a teenager again. Obviously, the next thing was for our two families to meet, so Tony began sorting out times and dates, when as many members of our family as possible could take time off to go to the USA. Eventually it was all set for June 1992 – Tony and I, Teresa, Pat and our Phil were booked and ready to go.

But then just before we left, we got a devastating call from America. Phil was dying. He'd been diagnosed with liver cancer and was only given two weeks to live at best.

This was not the kind of reunion we'd had in mind but it was clear there wasn't a moment to lose. We flew to the States, hired a car at the airport and drove as quickly as we could to the town of Chester where Phil now lived. We were surprised to see that Phil must have fallen on harder times in recent years. Once he'd been in his family's catering business and then he moved on to open his own car dealership. But now he'd ended up in a small house in a run-down part of town.

We found him, thin and pale, lying in a hospital-style bed, hooked up to a drip in the bedroom of the little house. But his face lit up when he saw us, and Helen, who was small and bubbly just like Rose, greeted us warmly.

While the men embraced and talked, Teresa, Pat and I went to speak to Helen. She'd been very understanding throughout the whole adventure, but deep down we felt it couldn't have been easy for her. This was a distressing time and to have another family with strong links to her husband suddenly appear out of nowhere must have been very difficult.

Teresa and Pat tried to raise this with her tactfully.

'Ah, what the hell,' said Helen, 'it was the war years! It happens. Here, take this and give it to your Nan.'

She fetched a lovely red lipstick and made Pat promise to give it to Rose when we got home. Tony got to visit his father twice and he was also introduced to other members of the Di Meglio clan, including Phil junior, his half-brother. They all agreed that Tony, with his dark good looks, fitted right in and was clearly part of the family.

Sadly Phil passed away on the last day of our holiday but for a man who'd been given barely a week to live, it was a miracle he managed to hang on for almost a month. It was as if he was determined to wait for us. It meant the world to Tony for the two of them to be able to meet and I reckon it did to Phil too. I was just so glad they'd found each other before it was too late.

∞CHAPTER 9∞

I'VE GOT A PRESENT FOR YOU BABE,' SAID TONY PROUDLY

Over the next few years we moved house twice more. As time passed and the children were growing up, we realised that the nearby market town of Leighton Buzzard offered a bigger choice of schools on the doorstep than we could reach from our small village. We loved Toddington but with four kids of varying ages and stages of education, it was time to be practical, so we started looking for a new home more convenient for getting them all to their different schools on time.

We found a house on a quiet, contemporary estate with wide grass verges and a friendly atmosphere, very similar to where we lived in Toddington but close to the town centre of Leighton Buzzard. It was ideal.

But while we were still house-hunting, the estate agent, in the way that estate agents do, sent us a property that was outside our price range and quite different from the sort of thing we'd requested.

It was an old cottage, on the opposite edge of town, surrounded by a large, private garden and tucked away almost out of sight behind a development of much newer properties. I fell in love with it immediately. There was something about the place and its peaceful setting that tugged at me. But of course there was no way we could afford it. So instead we made an offer on the sensible modern house and we were accepted.

Yet it's strange what fate has in store. A few years later, when all the children were needing secondary schools, we realised life would be easier if we relocated again to the other side of town where the 'big' comprehensives were. So we began house hunting once more and what should come up but the old tucked away cottage I'd been so drawn to previously.

The cottage was much the same, but this time we were different. Tony was doing very well in his business, our modern house had gone up in value and the cottage, nearly 100 years old, was beginning to need a lot of repairs which held its price down in comparison. To our amazement we realised we could afford it.

The windows were creaky, the roof needed mending, most of the rooms in the interior had been knocked into one – it was like a big open barn. Yet I loved it. It reminded me a bit of those picturesque little cottages you see in Suffolk. And the garden, complete with a tangle of tall, shady trees at the bottom, almost a small wood, was magical. I didn't want to live anywhere else.

'Could be a money pit.' people warned us, because of course it was true there was a lot of work to be done, but it didn't matter. From the moment we walked in the door and felt the warm, welcoming atmosphere, I knew this was the place for us.

We spent many happy years slowly renovating the cottage and garden. Tony even created a beautiful big pond outside the French windows, which he filled with fish, and then built a Japanese style bridge over it so we could look down and watch them swimming about. In the end they got so tame they'd take food from your fingers.

We loved to spend whole days out there, just pottering about or enjoying lively family meals in the open air. Often, when I wandered in the garden on my own, particularly in the early morning or evening, I caught a fleeting glimpse of a little girl in a Victorian style dress, always just whisking away as I turned to get a good look at her.

Years later we discovered that the young daughter of one of the first owners of the cottage had sadly drowned in a pond. This took place in the fields that surrounded the area a century before the new homes were built. Later still, I visited a medium and she told me the little girl and her father still visited the cottage frequently, and they were very pleased at the way we were taking care of the old place. I was quite sure that accounted for the happy atmosphere.

But then as the twentieth century drew to a close and the new millennium approached, we entered a sad time in our lives. Tony had felt unwell for quite a while and on our 35th wedding anniversary of all days, he was diagnosed with kidney cancer which turned out to be inoperable.

I won't dwell on this difficult time made even worse by the news that our son Phil, now grown up with a wife of his own, had just been told his new born son Callum had serious medical problems and was not expected to live. Most of the baby's organs were crammed into his little chest cavity and there was not much that could be done. The poor little mite passed away only a few months later.

It wasn't easy to look on the bright side with so much sadness in the house, but we did our best. Mammy and Daddy back in the old days in Ballyragget had coped with poverty, cold, hunger and hardships unimaginable today, by finding the joy and laughter in the most dire of situations – as did most of the people in the village. It was the only way to survive and I suppose their attitude rubbed off on me. Just like Uncle Neddy we searched for the humour whenever we could.

One day, while he was still able to get about, Tony went off in the car and returned a few hours later with a pile of great big boxes.

'Jesus Babe, what have you got there?' I asked as he staggered in.

'It's a present - for you.' he said proudly.

Intrigued, I followed him into the sitting room. I liked pretty clothes, flowers, pictures and interesting craftwork, as Tony well knew. I couldn't imagine what sort of present for me would come in a set of big, business-like boxes.

Tony started opening them up and out came a large, grey computer monitor, a keyboard and various chunky bits of kit with worryingly complicated looking trailing wires.

'For me?!' I said aghast. I'm the most non-technical person imaginable, I can't type, I don't get on with lots of buttons. Machines and me don't mix. Even the washing machine had been a challenge. 'You must be out of your mind Tony!'

But Tony just laughed. 'You'll soon get the hang of it Peg. And look!' he held up a small grey object. 'It's got a camera. You don't need any film, or to take it down to the chemists to get it developed. It's digital. You can take as many pictures as you like and look at them on the computer as often as you want. You'll be able to print them out too.'

'Maybe the kids could, I said, 'but not me! Never in a million years!'

'I'll teach you Peg. It's easy.'

I shook my head. I doubted I'd ever get the hang of that contraption but I didn't want to disappoint him. He was so pleased with his gift I didn't have the heart to tell him to take it back, as, it was a waste of money. So I let him play with the instructions and set it all up until the novelty wore off. Then we found a place for the new computer and camera, put them away and I hardly thought of them again for a very long time.

I realise now, of course, that this gift was of huge significance. Looking back I think Tony suspected he wasn't going to make it and he wanted to get me started with a new interest, some sort of hobby to keep me occupied in the lonely days ahead. He'd always been a bit psychic – maybe he sensed that this was the new path I needed to follow. At the time though, I just thought he'd been seized by a crazy impulse and that eventually, once a decent interval had elapsed, I could donate that computer to a charity shop.

After a very long and brave battle with kidney cancer, Tony passed away two years later in July 2002. It was a devastating time. He was the love of my life, the only man I'd ever looked at, adored by me since I was sixteen years old and I didn't know how I could manage without him.

Yet at the same time, I knew he wasn't gone completely. I could sense him still close by. I missed his physical presence, his handsome face and his reassuring voice and yet at times it felt as if he was walking beside me unseen, as if he was still involved in everything we were doing. I remembered that time all those years ago in Toddington when I'd watched Tony and Charlie and even my own body, from somewhere up near the ceiling. Maybe Tony was even now, looking down on me in just the same way. So naturally I talked to him, just as I always had done.

Tony had wanted to be cremated and of course after the service I had to decide what to do with his ashes which would take about three weeks to be ready for me.

'Babe, I was thinking of having you made into diamonds!' I told him one day – because there had been stories in the newspapers about a new process whereby a loved one's' ashes could be converted into beautiful diamonds. In some ways it was an appealing idea – creating something bright and precious out of my bright and precious man. 'I could wear you on my finger in a ring. What d'you think of that?' I asked him. 'I could keep an eye on you the whole time then!'

Yet somehow, it seemed to me Tony wasn't keen on that idea. If only you could answer me, so I'd know for sure, I thought.

'So what d'you want mum?' asked Phil who was organising everything. 'We could sprinkle the ashes in the garden of remembrance.'

I was horrified. 'No. I want him home, where he belongs.' 'But are you sure mum – really?' 'Of course.' I said, 'I've got to have him here with me.'

So I chose a beautiful wooden box – the finest money could buy - for the ashes to be stored in and waited for them to arrive.

It seemed like ages but eventually one day I came home from the shops to find Phil waiting indoors with strange look on his face.

'Are you feeling ok mum?' he asked.

'Course I am. Why wouldn't I be?'

'You sure? You're really feeling ok?'

'For heaven's sake Phil. What is this?' I asked.

'The ashes have arrived!'

My hand flew to my mouth, then I looked all round. No sign of the beautiful wooden box. 'He's home! But where is he?'

'He's in the cupboard.' said Phil.

'Jesus Phil! Take your father out of the cupboard!' I cried.

So Phil went to the cupboard and came back with a mundane cardboard box in his hands.

I stared at the dull container in complete horror. I was bitterly disappointed and quite angry. 'Oh my God, why have they put your father in a cardboard box?!' I cried and felt tears rushing back. The insult to my poor man, shoved into cheap cardboard like a packet of cornflakes.

'No mum,' said Phil hastily, 'that's just to keep it safe. The proper box is inside.'

And he opened the lid and drew out the beautiful wooden casket I'd chosen. What's more the wooden box was displayed inside a clear perspex box Phil had had custom made by his Uncle (in the perspex business), so as to protect it. Only the best was good enough for my Tony. What a relief. I took the box in my own hands and held it tightly. My Babe was back where he belonged.

Later, when we were alone, I put the boxes on my dressing-table. 'Well Babe.' I said, 'You're never going to get out of three boxes!'

For a while he sat in splendour on my dressing-table but then a new thought began to bother me. I'd chosen a very lovely box. It could easily be mistaken for a jewellery box and was in full view of the window should any intruder creep by.

'You know what Babe,' I said after reflecting for a while, 'I'm going to put you on top of the wardrobe in case there are burglars. Don't be offended.' And as I'm not very tall, I dragged out a chair and climbed up to put the precious box out of harm's way.

But after a while, even that began to bother me. Would the top of the wardrobe be too obvious a place I wondered? Wouldn't that be one of the first places to draw a burglar's eye once he'd got in? Maybe there was somewhere safer.

I looked round the room and my gaze fell on the en-suite, with its twin hand basins, that Tony had made for us at the end of the bedroom – perhaps this would be better. So I climbed up to the wardrobe again, retrieved the box and hid it away under the sink.

Not long afterwards the priest called. We'd asked him to conduct a little service for us to sprinkle the ashes in the garden Tony loved so much. But by the time the priest arrived it started to rain so hard I couldn't face it. I thought I can't lock my Babe out in the garden in that weather. I wouldn't be able to shut the door, so I called the ceremony off.

'That's alright Missus,' said the priest, quite understanding. 'But d'you mind my asking where you're keeping him at the moment?'

'On top of the wardrobe,' I lied. I didn't want anyone finding out the truth and saying disapprovingly, 'Look at his final resting place.'

What's more, I'd also got a visit to a spiritualist church planned but that had worrying implications too. 'Babe please don't say you're under the sink to a church full of people.' I begged. And fortunately he didn't.

Yet of course I still missed him. At first I couldn't sleep in our big double bed. It seemed so empty and lonely without him that for a while, I slept in the spare room with the light on. But one night I was lying there grieving when I heard the bedroom door open, the side of the mattress behind me went down as if a weight had sat on it and I felt a pair of strong arms wrap round me, real and solid and reassuring and I could feel the warmth of a head on the pillow beside mine.

'Babe that better be you!' I told him. But of course I knew it was Tony and it was so comforting to lie in his arms again, I drifted happily off to sleep.

A few weeks later I was back in our big bedroom one morning, cleaning our two hand basins. I never change Tony's sink – even now. His shaving brush is still there alongside his soap, just the way it always was. Anyway there I was scrubbing away at some greasy marks on my own sink when a movement caught my eye. I looked across at Tony's sink and saw that the shaving brush was moving, then the soap. Puzzled, I stared at them, wondering what could be doing it.

Then the whole room began to fill with light. I turned back towards the bed and my mouth just fell open. The whole area from floor to ceiling was getting brighter and brighter, filling with a radiance so dazzling it was hard to look at it. As I watched, the light seemed to gather and concentrate into one huge, glowing, egg shaped column that stretched from carpet to ceiling – a column so brilliant, the rest of the room just faded away into shadow. Then before my awestruck eyes, the column seemed to part in the middle and come open and - out walked Tony.

I gasped. It was Tony, as real and solid and healthy looking as he'd been a few summers ago before he fell ill. He was wearing his yellow checked shirt and beige trousers and he was carrying a child in his arms. He smiled at me and nodded down at the little boy he was holding. I looked closer and saw that it was Callum – our poor little grandson who'd passed away after a few short months. But not Callum as I remembered him, a tiny, thin little scrap, so poorly, but a rosy, strong, happy looking toddler – the gorgeous child he would have grown into by now had he lived.

'Oh my god babe – you're home!' I cried in delight. And I held my arms out to them in sheer joy.

Still carrying Callum, Tony walked towards my outstretched arms, a loving smile on his face. But just as he reached me, as I was about to put my arms around him and feel the soft fabric of his shirt and the firm muscles beneath against my skin – he vanished. He was gone, like smoke and I was holding empty air.

The radiance slowly faded, the light returned to normal and once again I was standing in the ordinary bedroom, arms outstretched, a cleaning cloth still dangling limply from my fingers.

I was absolutely overwhelmed. It was disappointing not to have hugged Tony of course, yet despite that, I felt good. That sharp, jagged feeling of loss inside, stuck there permanently like a piece of broken glass, was somehow calmed and stilled. I felt much, much better. My Tony was still there. He was close. I was quite right to talk to him because I knew he could hear me. It was ok. I could cope. If only he could find a way to answer....life would be almost bearable..

My youngest daughter Pat had been staying with me those first difficult weeks, but now I was feeling so much better, it was right that she should get back to her own husband and home. I was keen for her to get on with her life, but the day she was due to leave I couldn't help feeling a bit low. I'd miss her.

Realising this, Pat wracked her brains for something to cheer me up.

'I know mum. That camera Dad got you – we've never really tried it out. Let's work out how to use it.'

To be honest, I wasn't that interested. What would I want to be taking pictures for? Now that I was on my own what would I want to photograph anyway? But to please Pat I looked at the camera and computer and the whole complicated caboodle. Actually on closer inspection, I was surprised to see the camera looked pretty normal. Not much different to the non-digital affairs we'd owned over the years.

'Okay mum,' said Pat, 'Let's go out in the garden and I'll take a picture of you.'

So I followed her into the garden and stood myself beside the pond with the house in the background. Pat took herself a few yards off and began clicking away. After a while I was getting a bit bored. It was getting chilly and I've never liked standing about, posing. Suddenly Pat gasped. 'Oh my goodness! What's that?'

I looked up. 'What? Have you cut my head off?'

'No!' said Pat. 'No, something's come out on the picture. Above your head. Sort of mist.'

Since it was a bright, clear evening with not a hint of mist anywhere, this seemed unlikely unless there was something wrong with the camera. Pat came over and showed me the tiny digital screen. Sure enough, there I was standing in front of the house but directly above my head, where we both knew there had only been clear, empty air, you could see a dense cloud of mist.

'Let's take it inside and look at it bigger on the computer monitor.' said Pat.

So we went indoors and Pat rigged up all the equipment and a few minutes later she got the photograph up on the big screen. We both stared at it in amazement. It was me, in front of the fence, but over the top of me, looking down was a foggy outline.

'Oh my God.' said Pat, 'It's Dad's energy around you!' I stared at the image open mouthed. Maybe there was something in this photography business after all. 'Let me have a go of that camera Pat.' I said.

∞CHAPTER 10∞

INSTANTLY I WAS TRANSPORTED BACK TO THE RIVERBANK IN IRELAND

I stared at the picture on the screen in amazement. Now I'd got the hang of this digital camera lark I was quite enjoying taking pictures. In fact I kept getting the urge to jump up and take photos for no reason at all - and at any time of the day or night at that.

This particular evening my son Paul was securing something on the back of the house for me when I was suddenly seized with the need to take a picture of him. It was getting dark, there were no scenic views and Paul wasn't wearing or doing anything special, nevertheless I couldn't rest until I had photographed him.

I grabbed the camera, which was never far from my hand and rushed outside.

'Honestly Mum!' sighed Paul when he saw me appear, camera in hand and guessed what I was up to. But he stood obediently nevertheless. It was a clear, bright night with not a cloud in the sky and I clicked away happily for a minute or two. Then I looked down at the tiny screen on the back of the camera. It was very small, but I could just make out my picture – there was Paul, the wall of the house and a great swirl of mist descending from the sky over the top of him.

I looked up at the real scene. The sky was black still and you could see the first stars appearing. Not a trace of fog or smoke anywhere. Nothing at all to blur the solid figure of my son. Yet somehow the camera had recorded a cloud of mist, quite invisible to us standing there.

'Wow Paul!' I said, 'There's something going on here.'

Excitedly I took the camera indoors, and connected it to the computer monitor. Thank heavens for Pat showing me how and instantly the picture came out full size. It was breathtaking.

Instantly I was transported back to the riverbank in Ireland and my lovely magic lights. I just knew that these mysterious shapes were the same, only bigger. Instinctively I understood now that the lovely little balls of light weren't just natural phenomena like lightning or fire flies, though they were natural. They seemed to me to be people; the surviving personalities of people who'd passed away and no longer needed their old bodies to move them about. They existed now as pure energy – whooshing around wherever they chose in little chariots of light – seldom seen by the naked eye yet, for some reason able to be picked up by the impartial gaze of a camera.

Intrigued by this idea I did a search on Google and discovered that other people had photographed them too and there was even a name for them. They were called 'orbs'.

Well that did it. I just had to see more of them. I was fascinated to think that there was a whole invisible world out there, swirling around unseen at our fingertips - a world that could be made visible just by clicking a camera shutter. Then and there I decided I had to document it.

I began to take my camera everywhere with me. I photographed everything – though only when the sudden impulse struck – which was quite often. Indoors, outdoors, old churches, empty fields – it was amazing the secrets they revealed. Sometimes I'd be out driving and have to stop the car to capture part of a bridge or a roadside shrine. It soon became clear that my camera was picking up different sorts of 'orbs'. There were the beautiful, delicately coloured globes that I took to be people but also, out in nature there were other fabulous energies at work. The air above night-time cornfields turned out to be ablaze with streaks and ropes of golden light, while flower-beds and woods were alive with tiny winged shapes that looked like fairies or angels. The empty skies were actually teeming with life

My fascination just grew and grew. What a wonderful hobby Tony had unwittingly created for me.

'See what you've done Babe,' I said one day as I downloaded some fresh pictures onto the computer I kept in the bedroom. I was looking up at Tony's picture as I spoke. I'd had one of my favourite photos of Tony blown up large, framed and hung on my bedroom wall. It showed my darling man in that very same yellow and white checked shirt he'd been wearing the day he appeared in the bedroom with Callum in his arms.

Then I had an idea. 'If you can hear me Babe, give me a sign.' I said and I picked up the camera and took a couple of snaps of the bedroom wall. Quickly I checked the tiny screen. There, clear, shining and unmistakable, right on Tony's photo was a beautiful orb. He'd answered me.

At last! A wonderful feeling of relief and excitement rushed through me. I'd been talking to Tony for months, certain he was there but frustrated by his lack of response and now, at last, we'd found a way to communicate. It wasn't perfect of course. Tony was restricted to 'voicing' approval or disapproval or just confirming that he was there and knew what was going on, by the appearance or non-appearance of his orb – but it was wonderful nevertheless.

From then on we chatted all the time. On our wedding anniversary I put a rose and two glasses of champagne on a little table and took it out into the garden.

'There you are Babe,' I said, 'and you'd better drink that before I do.'

And I stood back and snapped the table. Then I turned the camera over to see if anything had come out. Sure enough, there right on the rim of one of the champagne glasses was an orb. He was here. I picked up my own glass and drank a toast with him just like we always did on our anniversary.

But it wasn't just Tony who came to be photographed. Visiting Ireland one summer I was out walking round our old family haunts with my brother Michael when we came to the street where Aunt Sarah used to live. To my disappointment as I stared up and down at all the houses, they looked different and I could no longer recognise my Aunt's old home.

'Oh Sarah,' I said out loud to her in case she was around, 'I'm looking back now but I just can't remember which house was yours.' And I took a picture of the whole street. When I checked the camera, there on the front door of one of the houses was a huge white orb.

'Jesus Peg,' said Michael when I showed him, 'That's amazing. I'm sure that's Sarah's house and there's not another orb anywhere in the picture.'

Sometimes there were sad stories attached. One day Michael and I were out taking pictures in the countryside and a local farmer came to see what we were doing. He was very interested in the strange things the camera was picking up.

'See that field down there?' he said, pointing out a grassy meadow across the lane that led down to a brook. 'See what you get there.'

Puzzled, Michael and I set off through the buttercups. I didn't know where to start – it was a big field, but after a minute or two I felt drawn to a place where a small bridge crossed the water. I took a few photographs of it and as I stood there, my feet sinking into the soft ground, a terrible feeling of sadness began to wash over me.

Back by the farmer we reviewed the pictures. They were all empty except the ones by the bridge which showed two, pure white orbs side by side and very close, hovering over the grass.

The farmer stared at them in silence for a long time. Then at last, he spoke.

'A few years back, during the troubles, the IRA came for two boys from the village. Best friends they were. The men said they were informers or traitors or something and took them away. We found their bodies next day, just there by the bridge – just where those orbs are. They'd been shot.'

Something similar happened back in England. Driving regularly to my local shopping centre in Milton Keynes, I noticed one day that a little crucifix had appeared at the side of the road, pushed into the grass on a bend. Beside the cross was a beautiful bunch of fresh flowers. Sights like this have become increasingly common, in our area at least, and I realised it must mark the spot where there'd been a fatal accident.

I went past it often and every time I drove by, I noticed the flowers had been replaced. Someone was working hard to make sure their loved one always had fresh flowers. Then one wet morning I drove past and there it was again with yet another bunch of perfect blooms. I did my shopping and came back. The rain was pelting down even harder, spray was flying off the road and all I wanted to do was get home and put the kettle on. Yet there was the little shrine again, the petals drooping and mud splashed now, so forlorn somehow in the storm. As I skimmed by, the image stayed in my mind. I couldn't get it out of my head.

The further I drove, the more it nagged at me. In the end I couldn't stand it any longer. I turned the car round and went back. I pulled up alongside the shrine. I had my camera with me of course but it was raining so hard I didn't want to get out, so I wound down the window and photographed the little scene.

When I looked at the picture, there on top of the crucifix was a huge orb, absolutely enormous – like the moon. And from somewhere I heard a voice murmur: 'I'm Jason. I was on a bike…Tell my parents it wasn't my fault.'

If only I could I thought. But I've no idea how to find them….

Often though, the orbs were comforting or even amusing. Occasionally they came in so strongly I could see them myself without even using the camera. One night I was at home getting ready for bed when I clearly saw a big black orb drift across the ceiling. I'd never seen a black orb before and the colour was quite unsettling. What's more it looked really solid, not ethereal and transparent as they usually appear.

I stared at it uneasily as it hovered above the bed. Then as I watched, an inner glow seemed to illuminate it, it grew and changed shape then the sides seemed to split open and Uncle Neddy's face appeared black and grubby and grinning, the way he always looked when he'd been out turf cutting.

'Jesus Neddy!' I cried, 'You frightened the life out of me. Haven't you washed your face yet?'

Neddy's grin got wider and then the orb slowly drifted away and vanished through the ceiling – for all the world like that Santa Claus mask all those years ago. Dear old Neddy, I thought and I climbed into bed with a warm, affectionate feeling. They were still close my loved ones – all of them.

They even seemed to have a wonderful ability of keeping me out of danger. Pat was now married to a lovely man called Kevin and they'd moved to the coastal town of Felixstowe in Suffolk. I often went to stay with them and Pat and I had fallen into the habit of driving out to a favourite area of the seafront and taking an evening stroll along the beach. Orbs always show up better in the dark and the orbs that appeared in the night sky above the waves were spectacular – a truly beautiful sight. We never tired of photographing them.

But one particular night in very early March 2008, we parked the car and went down to the beach, as usual and got nothing. I took frame after frame, I asked the spirit people to come and give us a sign but not a single orb appeared on the pictures.

'Come on lads (I always call them lads)' I said in disappointment, 'Where are you?'

There was no reply. The sky stayed resolutely dark and empty. Admittedly it was quite windy and the sea was rough but the weather had never put them off before.

'This is weird Pat,' I said at last, 'I can't understand it. But we're obviously wasting our time here. Let's go down to the old fishing village and see if we have better luck there.'

So we went back to the car and drove on to the fishing village. We re-parked beside the picturesque ancient buildings and tried again. Immediately, lovely orbs began to appear all over the sky.

'That's very odd Pat.' I said, 'They're here so I can't understand why they didn't want to appear on the beach.'

But we got loads of pictures and then went home. At least the evening wasn't wasted after all.

Next morning though, Pat rushed in, her face astonished yet excited. 'Mum you'll never believe this,' she said, 'the sea broke through the sea wall last night and the waves crashed on to the prom right where we were! It took some beach huts and also brought down the power cables right near where we would have been standing! The biggest waves for ten years they say – we might have been killed!'

My mouth fell open. That explained it. That was the reason the lads refused to come when we were on the beach. They led us to the fishing village on purpose I realised, to keep us out of harm's way.

Over the years Pat became as interested in the magical orbs as I was, but being young and clever, she was always looking on the internet to see if she could find out more about them. Always eager to learn, Pat began to realise that the orbs weren't just intriguing local phenomena for us and our family. But that there were other people out there getting similar results and there was international interest.

'Mum,' she said one day, 'I've got a confession to make. I've entered you for something in the USA – and you've been accepted. How d'you feel about going to Palm Springs?'

I was stunned. 'What? Palm Springs? What have you entered me for? You must be out of your mind!'

Pat began to explain. Apparently there was this organisation in America devoted to investigating spiritual phenomena and they held a conference every year called the Orbs and Prophets Conference. For their 2008 conference, they'd invited people from around the world to submit their own photos of orbs and the organisers were going to invite the best eight entrants to come to the conference, show their pictures and give a talk.

'I sent them some of your pictures mum,' Pat said nervously, 'and you've been accepted. I've told them you'll come and talk to the conference.'

For a moment I thought I might pass out. How could I possibly get up on a stage and talk to an audience? I couldn't do that in a million years. I was just a simple Irish girl with very little education – there was no way I could manage public speaking.

But Pat went on and on. I couldn't back out now she said. They were expecting me. And anyway it was the pictures they wanted to see, not me. It would be like a slide show with my pictures projected on a big screen. All I'd probably have to do was stand unseen at the side and just tell them where the pictures were taken. I owed it to the lads to let them be seen by more people.

Well I don't know how she did it, but Pat persuaded me. I asked Tony if he thought I should go, and a great big bright orb materialised instantly on his photo. It was clear he did. I began to understand that the pictures I was being given by my spirit visitors weren't just for my own personal comfort and entertainment. They were to be shared and it was time I started getting them out into the world to be seen by those open minded enough to want to see them.

So by mid to end March in 2008 I ended up in Palm Springs. Never would I have thought I would ever come back to this amazingly beautiful place without Tony. Just like my holiday with Tony and Pat years before, it was still the most beautiful city, with lovely blue sunny skies, palm trees everywhere, views of the distant mountains from every street and clear, sparkling dry air. I loved it!

What would Tony have thought all these years on? He would never have believed I could do this and the irony that it would be back to Palm Springs, California of all places!

As Pat was a full time Mum with Ruby at that time, a demanding toddler and Tony, who was just over a year old, she couldn't come along, so my son-in-law Kevin accompanied me instead.

As soon as we arrived, we dropped our suitcases at the hotel and went straight to the conference hall. We'd been told we were allowed to go and have a look at it in advance to prepare ourselves for the next day and I was desperate to see what I was letting myself in for.

The hall was only a short walk from the hotel. It was a handsome modern building, all glass interspersed with tall, rough stone pillars reminiscent of Stonehenge. Impressed, Kevin and I went inside and crossed a plush foyer that led to the main hall. Kevin opened the door.

To my horror I saw a huge room with row upon row of seats curving round a big stage, with more tiers of seats in a gallery above. The place must have held at least 2,000 people.

'It's not too late to turn round and get back on the plane!' joked Kevin.

I was tempted but I knew I couldn't. 'We can't go now.' I said, 'The lads are here.'

Because I'd asked them not to let me down, to stay close and Tony had assured me that they would, and I would be fine. All I had to do was be myself. No airs and graces. Just tell them about my pictures, plain and simple and I'd get all the help I needed. I couldn't let them down now.

And of course he was absolutely right. The next day I was a nervous wreck. I hardly slept all night and I couldn't eat a thing. But once I got up on that stage and looked out at all those faces, they seemed to blur into one, friendly group. A great wave of encouragement and affection seemed to roll out towards me from the audience and behind me, I could feel warmth and confidence coming from the lads. All the help I needed was there. So, I took a deep breath, opened my mouth and began to speak. I hadn't really known what to say, but as my old familiar pictures began to appear on the screen, the words just flowed and the audience seemed to be listening intently.

Afterwards there was a big roar of applause and I walked off stage feeling ten feet tall. The relief that it was all over and I'd managed it, was fantastic.

'Let's go and get some air Kevin!' I said as I got outside. But as we walked across the foyer, a man was coming down from the gallery upstairs. He looked up, saw us and hurried over.

'Excuse me ma'am,' he said, 'But I was very interested in your talk just now. I'm intrigued by those lights and I wanted to ask you something. I'm a long haul pilot and me and my co-pilot, we often see lights like the ones you've just been showing us, round the nose of the plane when we're flying. They appear and then they go again. We've both put in reports to the airline about it and asked what they were, but we never get any response.'

How interesting, I thought. Even thousands of feet up in the sky, orbs were still visible.

'Well you know, I should think those orbs are a good thing,' I said, 'I reckon they're protection. They're your loved ones or the loved ones of the passengers on the plane, surrounding you and keeping you safe. When you see those orbs you'll know you're protected and you're going to land safely.'

The pilot seemed very pleased with this explanation. 'And ma'am, I hope this isn't an imposition but could you possibly take a picture of me?'

Naturally I had my camera with me so we went out into the garden, stood him by a flowering bush and I took a photograph. When we checked it afterwards there was a big orb beside him and within the orb I could make out a misty figure.

'It looks like a woman in a rocking chair,' I said squinting at the tiny screen, 'She's wearing a white dress and a bonnet and she's holding her hands out like this.' And I demonstrated.

'That's my grandmother!' said the pilot in delight, 'She always sat like that and that's the kind of thing she wore.'

So we took his email address and promised to send him a copy of the picture when we got home. And so, despite my fears, Palm Springs turned out to be a wonderful experience.

That was 2008 and since then there have been thousands and thousands more pictures. I've been learning more and more and developing in new directions including healing. But that's for another book. For now, let me show you some of my favourite pictures from across the years......

~My Magic Lights~

~ - 93 - ~

This wonderful image is my favourite photo of them all!
It was taken at Borley Rectory, on the Suffolk, Essex borders on
7th August 2009 at 8:21pm. Some will see this as a Crucifix,
others as an Angel. I just think it is beautiful!

∞CHAPTER 11∞

SO WHAT IS AN ORB?

In the early days it was always very frustrating to me that 'orbs' seemed to be, by so many, discounted as mere particles of dust, or droplets of moisture in the air and picked up on the lens. But, even back then, I knew there was a whole lot more to orbs than met the eye, so to speak. To me, they were WAY more than random specks of dust (though, of course, there will always be a few that are just particles of dust caught on the lens). However, these will also have no definition inside them and will appear flat and one dimensional. In fact I've now come to believe that the majority of orbs are emanations of energy brought back to us by our loved ones who've passed on into the spirit world.

Years ago, I had to be wary of what I said in public. If I happened to mention the 'orb phenomena', especially whenever it came out in conversation that I was getting 'orbs' on my camera, I often got the same response - a blank expression, followed by a rapid change of subject. I got used to this topic of conversation automatically being dismissed, and I have to admit, it was disheartening to say the least.

At the time, I just accepted that people had always been afraid of what they didn't understand, and shied away from the subject. Yet it seemed odd to me, that given, for example, we know we cannot see radio waves, which carry billions of mega bytes of data and images through infrared radiation, via x-rays and gamma rays, somehow these are automatically accepted and not questioned and yet orbs were. It all seems bizarre to me! To me, it is simple, orbs and their manifestations are just energies on a higher vibrational frequency.

~My Magic Lights~

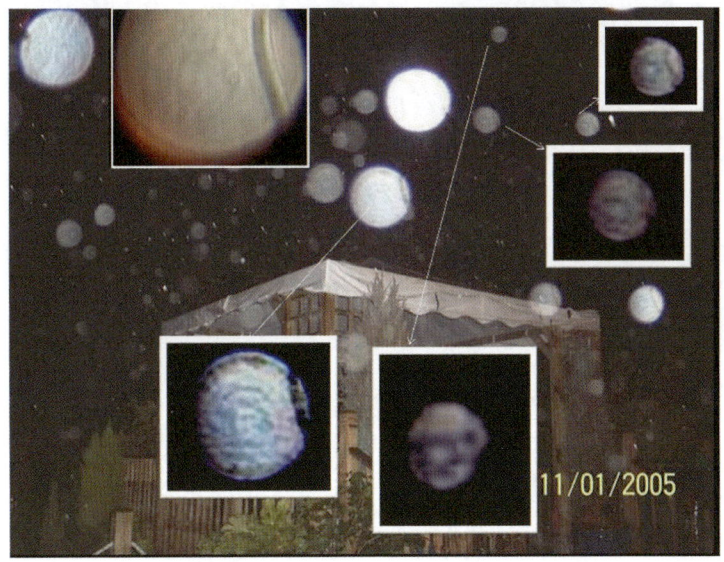

~ - 95 - ~

Note the vast collection of amazing and brilliantly vibrant orbs above, from this picture taken in my sister's garden in Ireland. The second photo, shows incredible detailed faces in some of the orbs above.

Scientists have been looking into the area of orbs and digital cameras and if you look anywhere on the web, it is still claimed orbs are relatively new and arrived with the digital era.

I personally do not believe this to be true and I have a few of my own examples of orbs taken on an old Polaroid Camera going right back to the 1970's and eighties.

The above photo of me was taken at home in Suffolk in 1971 with little Pat. And the orb above my right shoulder is visible (though not so in print) against our trendy orange wall paper!

The second picture is one I took of Tony and his mum Rose dancing at a family wedding in the eighties.

Orbs can come in many guises and I have included just a sample in this book taken from my vast collection spanning well over a decade. To break it down, each area has been categorized into the following title headings.

It has been very hard to get the quality of the images in the correct format for an acceptable 'print' quality. Disappointingly, when I received the first proof copy, nearly all the images were too dark, which we have read is a common problem.

Therefore each of the images have had to be slightly lightened. You will notice some of the images have been 'zoomed in', which has been a necessity to show a better detailed view. To do this, we have used Microsoft PowerPoint, using just the contrast and cropping tools. I am very protective of my images and do not want to use any other super editing suites available to enhance my pictures in anyway, as I feel this would not be a true and sincere way of representing myself or spirit. Furthermore, I really feel the images speak for themselves!

Evidence Orbs: I believe that our loved ones are constantly trying to let us know that they are still near us and still a part of our lives.

So they try to prove their presence by bringing their energy close to an object associated with them such as a photo, or a personal possession. This energy can be picked up by the camera for us to see in the form of an orb.

We can even have a conversation by asking the loved one questions and requesting that they produce an orb if they agree. Tony and I often have long chats using this method!

Orbs can also come through in stunning vivid colours. Sometimes, to indicate the identity of the loved one. For instance, when my sister Celia was alive, we would always joke that being Irish, she would emanate her energy as the colour green. That's exactly what she did after she passed over to spirit. Also, my daughter actually gets only one kind of orb when she talks directly to her Dad in spirit. *(See example photo in Chapter 13).* He always manifests as a rugby ball shaped orb. So evidence orbs can tailor their appearance to their audience to ensure a really personal link that gives huge reassurance to those left behind.

Children and Orbs: Children can easily bring in spiritual energy as, whilst they are young, they are so open minded. In Chapter 13, 'Grand Children Race with their Grandad', you will see some fantastic photos of the evidence given.

Sacred Sites: Following on from the first chapter in this book, where I detailed my visions as a child, over the years I've photographed many religious sites and been amazed at the orbs and entities that have been captured on camera.

I feel there is very special connection to a more pure, divine energy in holy grounds. Like my Dad, I've never been much of a one for organized religion but in sacred sites there's no doubt that something special lingers on. This, to me makes my 'religious' images more special, personal, real and true.

Healing Energies and Misty Images: As well as energies from orbs, there are some amazing healing energies, in which love and healing are brought to us by our past loved ones, along with, in some instances healing guides. This is one area I have always had a natural tendency to follow. Over the last decade, very sadly we have lost many dear family members to cancer. Having been so involved with nursing on the practical side of dealing with cancer, it has drawn me even closer to the spiritual side of 'healing'. Not only has this brought me lots of confidence, I now also realize this is the main area of spirituality that I would like to dedicate the time I have left. Nothing can beat the kind of healing, peace of mind and comfort to those who are in need of healing or for those who have recently lost their loved ones.

~My Magic Lights~

Nature Spirits and Luminosities: As a child I believed in fairies. I grew up with my family always telling stories of these delightful little creatures. Little did I know I would be capturing them on camera myself many years on. These brilliantly coloured little energies usually rise from the ground and stay in groups in my experience.

More about these and luminosities will be detailed in my next book!

∞CHAPTER 12∞

EVIDENCE ORBS & MY QUESTIONS ANSWERED THROUGH THE LENS

After a long procrastination to decide what would be the best colour to paint the walls, my son and I just couldn't agree, so he thought I was mad, when I said, 'let's ask your father!' Low and behold Paul couldn't believe the result after I took just one quick photo to decide. We then went with the sage green and Paul couldn't argue!

....As Tony still has the final say on the decorating!

Tony's token of love on our Wedding Anniversary:

Anniversaries can be very sad days when we miss our dearly departed loved ones. There are many occasions when I speak with Tony, and he will always give me a sign to prove he is there with me. On our wedding anniversary, I set up to a table with a glass of wine next to Tony's photo, to toast our special day. 'Can you drink it faster than I can babe?' I asked him. Immediately Tony's energy came through next to his photo frame.

The second photo above shows his energy on the champagne glass. I felt such comfort seeing this because I knew it was Tony giving me a sign on the glass, as if to confirm he was with me in his way of celebrating, with champagne, just like the old days.

I told Tony there is a lot more to spirits then he realised!.....

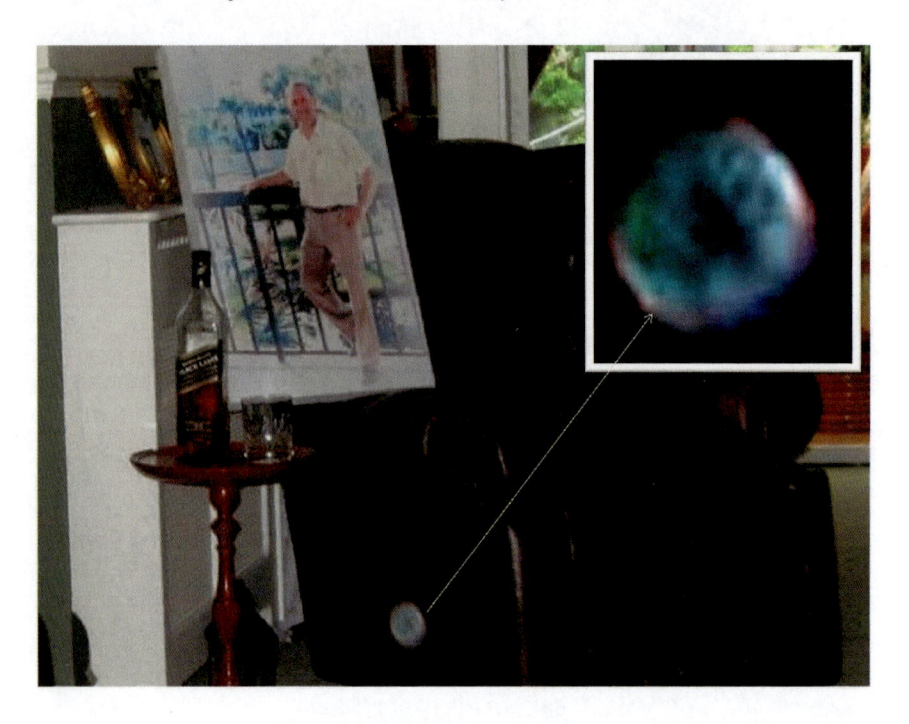

On Tony's birthday, he always enjoyed a drop of whiskey! On this occasion, I put his favourite crystal glass out, but I didn't have his favourite brand of whiskey, so I didn't think he would approve. I asked if he minded and this was the result!

My Magic Lights

~ - 103 - ~

I love these two images above clearly demonstrating Tony's love and affection given on the photo frame and then in the second photograph, his energy on the rose, sent back to me.

OTHER SIGNS OF EVIDENCE CAUGHT ON CAMERA:

The sheer colour, vibrancy and detail in this image to me is striking resemblance to that of Emma Hardinge Britten, famous Spiritualist Medium credited with defining the seven principles of Spiritualism, and still used today across the Spiritualists National Union of Churches, (SNU).

Interestingly, a few months earlier, whilst staying with friends in Market Harborough, she also appeared to me with such clarity. The detail of her amazing full length Victorian dress and loosely plaited hair, as she sat at the end of my bed. It wasn't long after this, I was invited to a Spiritual Church in Bedford and as soon as I walked in, right on the top of a pile of books was a magazine called 'Two Worlds', which I had never heard of before and it featured the same image again of Emma Hardinge Britten.

Striking resemblance to the image of Emma Hardinge Britten.

❧My Magic Lights❧

~ - 105 - ~

Here's Pat larking around one Halloween in the garden trying to catch her brother out, who was unaware she was hiding behind the trees, (complete with a terrifying Hannibal Lecter mask on to scare him)!

Though, little did she know what I was looking at her on the camera, which I noticed after taking this snap shot. This face seems to be looking down on Pat from the sky and it was as if to say, 'BOO'!! 'Now you get scared!'

Pat and I were playing some old vinyl 45 rpm records on the vintage
record player. At the time this photo was taken, I was thinking back
to how my parents loved this record and whilst I was talking about
these memories, we were playing 'Ave Maria' by Mario Lanza, I had
the feeling to take a sudden picture, unaware that this beautiful face
would result.

My Magic Lights

~ - 107 - ~

Attending an evening with Tony Stockwell (renowned Psychic Medium) in Felixstowe and despite being a little late and flustered, as we ran from the car park, I still felt the need to take a very quick photo. We hurriedly approached the large tree beside the entrance in the grounds of the hotel, when this remarkable image of a clear and seemingly very gentle face was the result.

In this incredible photo there is a very clear face (that I hope comes through as clear in print as it does on my camera).

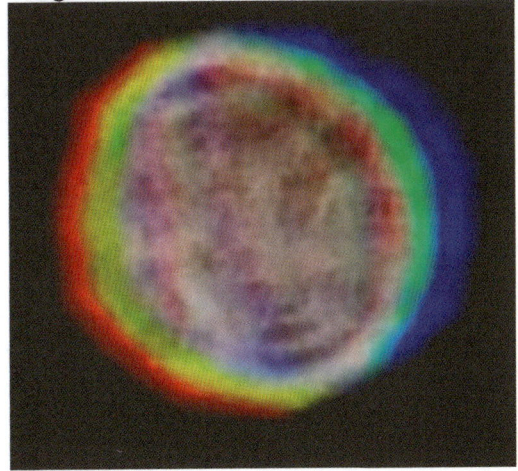

I felt compelled for some reason to take a photo of an area of my room, following a tapping sound I heard shortly before. I took the photo and didn't think anything of the results at the time. Little did I know this was going to be something that was going to become important.

A good few weeks on, I went to see a medium for a reading. She told me she had a lady come through who gave her name as Hinara, (I was so surprised as this was the name of my great grandmother from County Clare, Ireland). She says that you should look back in your recent photos, as she has shown herself.

This was the photo which I looked back on, shocked at the level of detail I missed before, with the Victorian hat and fancy décolletage! How did I miss this amazing clear image?!

Great Grandmother

∞CHAPTER 13∞

THE GRAND CHILDREN RACE WITH THEIR GRANDAD!

There is lots of talk about 'new age' children being described as 'Indigo' Children. These children are believed to possess special, unusual and sometimes supernatural traits or abilities. A concept developed in the 1970's by Nancy Ann Tappe. These children are particularly sensitive and much more tuned in and aware of the spirit world. They are also empathetic, curious and strong-willed. There are a lot more characteristics and I realize, not only do they match those of our little grandson, Tony, but I also see a lot of these traits in myself as well!

In her book, Nancy Tappe goes into the characteristics of an Indigo child in a lot more detail. The book is called 'Indigos, - The Quiet Storm', where Nancy groups the Indigo person in to four types, Humanist, Artist, Conceptualist and Catalyst.

This leads me on to the many occasions we have all witnessed or heard of a parent disregarding their child's experience with 'imaginary' friends, as just a figment of their imagination. Instead, I feel parents should quiz their children more and taken an active interest into this subject. If we really listen to our children, they can come out with remarkable statements which would melt the heart of even the most cynical adult! Indigo children seem to know things they couldn't possibly know and be way ahead of their years.

Some of the early signs as an example, was when my daughter would be alone with Tony, whilst changing his nappy in his room. He would suddenly stop gurgling and be distracted by something. His eyes would wander the ceiling, transfixed on something moving around. Even when my daughter was talking to him she could not get his attention, as he was more interested in interacting with someone else in the room. I am sure it would have been his grandad Tony, who he unfortunately didn't get to meet.

There have been so many instances with the grandchildren and one I particularly recall, was when Tony was about four years old when he often talked about grandad in his 'window'. On this occasion he was staying the night (which he often did in my room), and in the morning, he would wake me by prizing open my eye with his little short finger, and hurriedly get me to grab my camera. He would then excitedly, look around the room to see if he could spot grandad in his window! (orb). One time I humoured him to try and find out more. He got quite impatient and stamped his little foot in defiance, whilst bluntly pointing out, that I had been too late, as there was now a different grandad. I asked what this different grandad looked like. Tony described someone who was resting his chin in his hand with his fingers on his mouth and his legs crossed, I just instantly knew he was describing my dad!

So imagine how I feel seeing a grandson of mine being more accepted and able to talk about his experiences, something I was forbidden to do, except in the presence of my own mother and grandmother.

We once took a family holiday to Devon and our little Tony came down the stairs with a real look of concentration on his face, with his blanket snuggled up to his mouth. We all looked amazed at the sight of this little toddler trying to recite the words to the Beatles, recording 'No Where Man'. He got the words He's a 'real nowhere man' and hummed in between for the words he could not recite. Nobody had ever sang that song to little Tony and we were sure he had not heard it before.

But little did he know, it was one of his granddad's favourites in the '60's. Pat asked him where he had heard the song before. In his usual blunt and a matter of fact way, Tony replied, 'just now in my other ear'.

On another occasion Pat was worried about their family cat who wasn't himself. She was getting the children their breakfast and was thinking about the piece she had recently read in the local paper about cats drinking anti freeze and dying as a result of developing kidney failure.

In deep thought, she carried on in the kitchen, when Tony stead fast looked up at her and plainly remarked, 'don't worry Mummy, Kasey won't get kidney failure'. Pat was in shock on two counts, that Tony seemed to have read her mind and also the fact that being so young, he could even say the words kidney failure, so eloquently! When she asked why he said that, he said, 'I can read your mind when you get worried'.

One morning out of the blue Tony just casually said he wanted to race grandad to see who was the fastest. He chose his starting block at one side of the room and actually directed me where to stand to get the best shot, as if we were in some film studio! He flew through the air and with all the excitement, Ruby ran into the room not wanting to be left out! Ever since, the racing game with grandad has been a much anticipated regular feature with the kids when coming to nanny's house.

Note two orbs in this photo with Tony reaching up. It is as if his grandad is helping him reach his frame, by holding him up.

I love it when I get this evidence, especially when the grandchildren are interacting with their grandad and they are so matter of fact about it. There have been odd occasions, where the kids have done a little drawing or a note for Tony. As they go to attach it to his picture on the wall, low and behold he always shows he is acknowledging their presence.

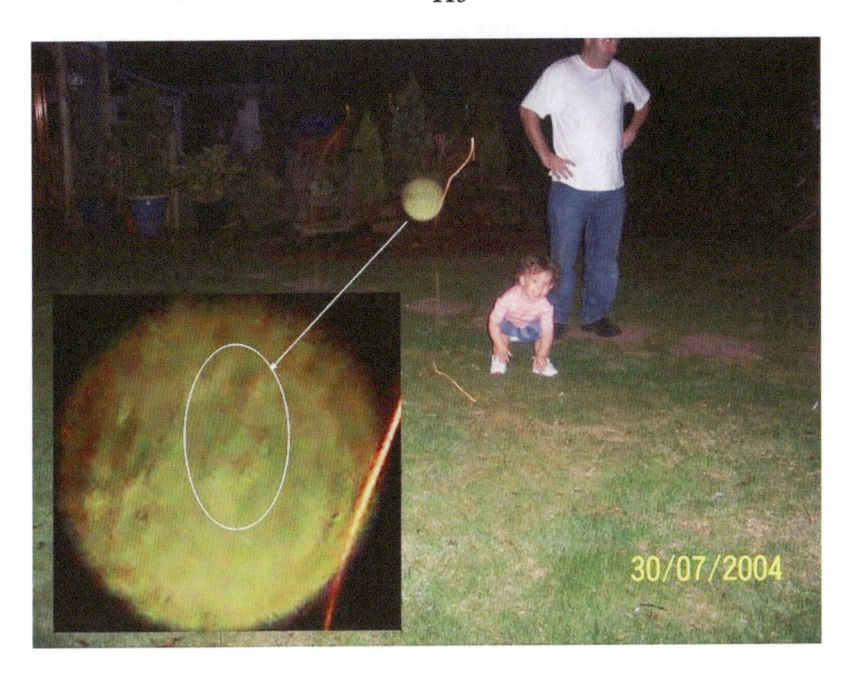

This photo was taken in my garden and shows our son Phil and our little granddaughter, Jaide. This beautiful orb must have manifested for them, to show a clear image of her grandad holding our little grandson Callum, also in spirit.

Note the orb in Tony's sink right in front of our grandson and the other one appears right on his hand.

Note the stunning vibrant pink energy in this photo. It is as if evidence has been given, by spirit they acknowledge it being Ruby's turn to race this time!

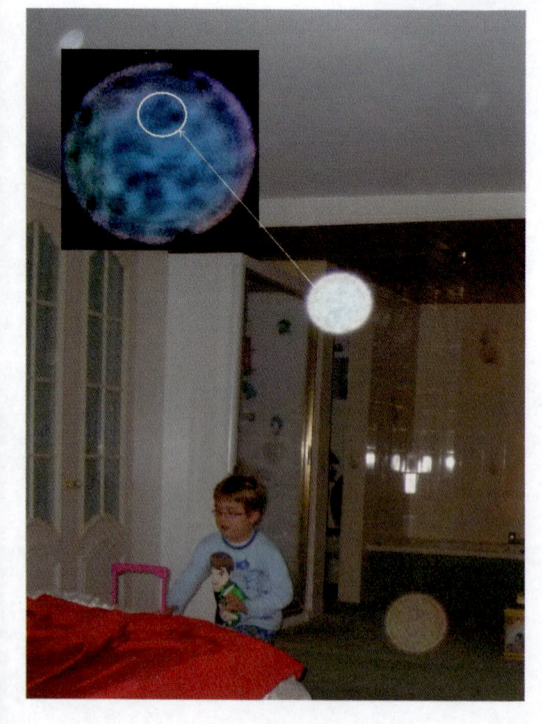

The picture afterwards shows the sheer abundance of orb energies coming in, as Tony bets he could run faster than grandad!

Below Tony's energy manifesting as a rugby ball shaped orb for my daughter, who is showing little Tony his grandad's photo.

A wonderful photo in its own right of Tony's image on a canvas next to the grandaughter he never met. So Pat and I just loved the evidence given with this orb landing directly on Ruby's head! I can just imagine Tony kissing Ruby's head when this was taken.

∞CHAPTER 14∞

SACRED SITES

I felt it was very important, whilst writing this book to include my most precious picture of them all. Imagine how I felt after seeing religious figures as a child, to now actually getting my own image on camera of the Crucifix!

Back in 2009, two dear friends of mine, Harry and Beryl Phillips from Suffolk, took me to visit the very old remains of what is still known as the 'most haunted house in England', on the Essex/Suffolk borders, namely, Borley Rectory, made famous by the writings of Harry Price.

In his book, Harry details the story of a Reverend's wife, named Marianne Foyster, who moved into the Rectory in October 1930. Marianne seemed to attract rapping's, noises, moving objects from spirit, until finally pleas of help were written on the wall, seemingly from spirit, as the hand-writing was unrecognizable.

Marianne decided to try and write a message back, stating she didn't understand. It then later transpired that in the late 1800's a Nunn named Marie Lairre, had left her convent to marry a man from a wealthy family. It was rumoured that her husband had strangled her and buried her alive within the walls of Borley Rectory. As it was purported that Marie Lairre's spirit couldn't rest, it was said she continued to haunt the rectory.

Harry Price stuck with the investigations and even camped outside Borley Rectory, whilst numerous reporters were drafted in to witness these etchings on the wall. Much later on, a fire ravaged the whole of Borley Rectory, and small bones were found. These were believed to be those of the young Nunn murdered by her husband. She was then given a Christian burial two miles away in the village of Liston.

Not aware of any of the history, when we arrived at Borley Rectory, I was very excited just knowing that I would be visiting a very ancient church! However, on arrival we realized it was locked! I was so very disappointed, so we had a quick walk around the graveyard and started to head off home.

On the exit from the church, there was a very narrow bridge across the river. As we were leaving, half way across the bridge, I had the most amazing feeling to get out of the car and take a picture and with a sense of urgency, I asked Harry to stop the car. Of course this must have sounded bizarre to my two friends, but Harry did stop the car and I snapped my camera. It wasn't until we got back to their house, that I was able to review the picture and low and behold, we were all truly astounded at the result!

Above is my most special and precious photo ever given to me by spirit!

The photo that follows is another special one I hold dear to my heart.

This image is one of the images shown on the front cover of this book and Michael and I both agree it is image of our Grandad.

Along with my brother Michael, very late one evening we visited our local cemetery, known as Donoughmore. This photo was taken late in the pitch black darkness. However, towards the entrance of the cemetery, a white mist started forming in front of us, just as I took this photo

I said out loud, 'we are home lads'. Aren't you coming to meet us?' We certainly didn't expect this image coming over the fence, when we reviewed the photo on the camera! Our grandad!

Throughout my life I have always had such a high regard for spirit, as I have always loved and respected them, knowing they are just our loved ones who have gone on before us.

My brother and I went to my Father's grave that evening and I just felt I had to take a few pictures of the grave stone, 'The Family Chains are broken now, and nothing seems the same, but as God calls us one by one, the links shall join again, is the inscription.

The photo, reflects the words of the poem, showing the links are broken with the next showing the links are clearly joined!

Our body carries our 'souls' throughout our lives but on our death this 'vehicle' is no longer required and our souls lives on in a much higher realm when we all go on, one by one and will all see for ourselves the familiar faces of our past loved ones waiting to greet us.

I love the inscription on my Father's grave with the wording: 'The Family Chains are broken now; nothing seems the same, but as God calls us one by one, the chain will link again'.

Poem by Author, Ron Tranmer.

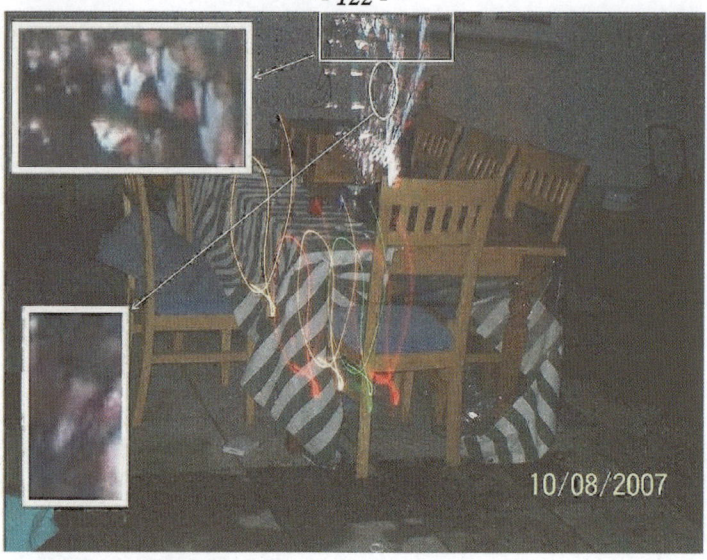

During a family gathering, we were playing music in my brother's garden. Not thinking anything special would come of it, I took this photo. Amazingly it seemed to depict a gathering of people at an old fashioned funeral. Zooming in on the central image, it is quite clear there are people wearing funeral attire. Very interestingly, one of them is clearly the image of a man, adorned with a trilby hat and 'grandad' shirt, reminiscent of the style of the 1930's era.

Below are some of the typical greetings I receive inside a Church.....

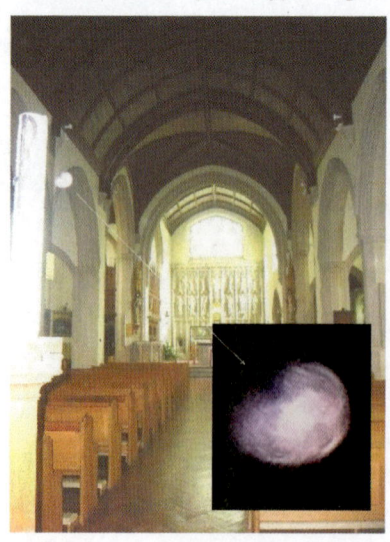

Peggy Weber

~ - 123 - ~

Some more heart warming signs I get when I enter a Church.

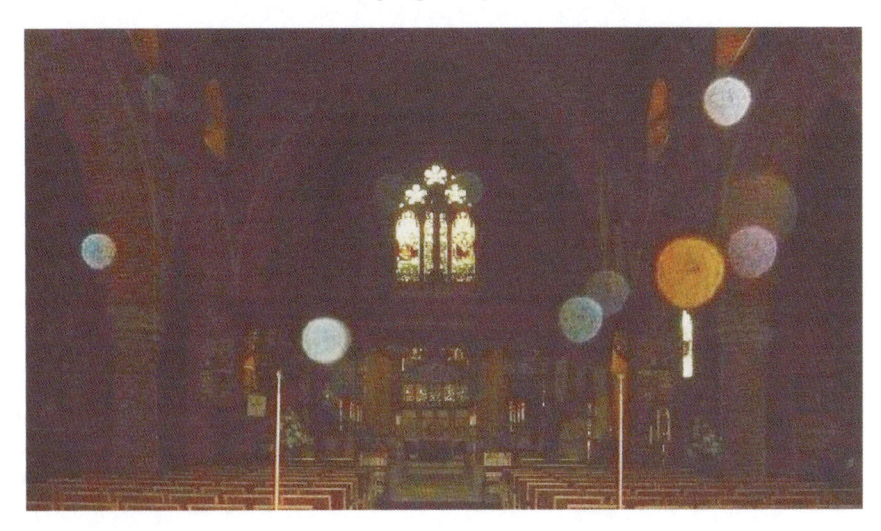

Below is a wonderfully comforting image. This was taken during one of my usual Church visits. I was holding out a rose for our very much missed family members now in spirit. A very comforting result!

The photos below are just amazing to see. Firstly, from no presence at all in the first photo, then in the second a split second later, a mist can be seen clearly approaching the statue of Jesus.

Then the image of a lady, quite clearly, in a blue dress with her hair pinned up. My lovely niece Sarah, now in spirit, loved St. Etheldreda, so this image, does make me wonder.

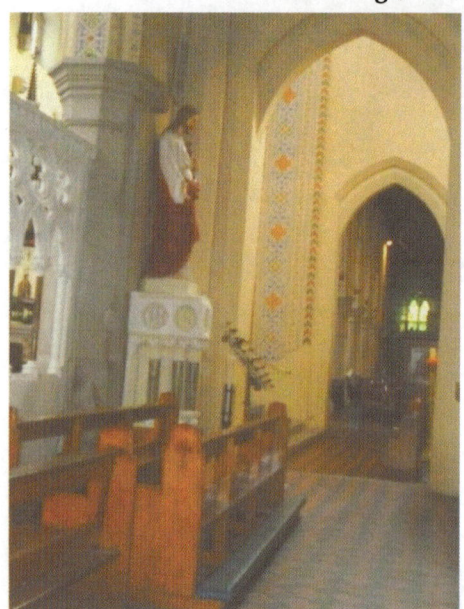

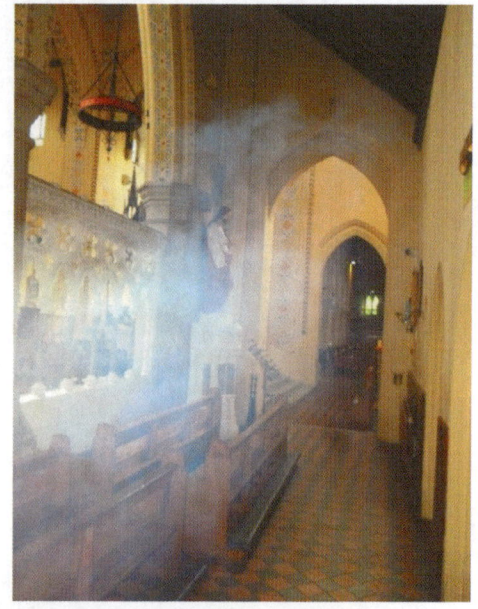

∞CHAPTER 15∞

JOURNEY FROM ORBS TO HEALING

A dear friend of mine Robert Allen, requested healing wishes on his social networking page, for a close friend of his who was ill at the time. He announced that he would appreciate help from other healers, located in various parts of the country. To do this they would all concentrate their healing thoughts and wishes at the same time that evening.

With this in mind, I went out to gather a bunch of daisies. I then made a circle with them in the garden on the grass, with a little

tea-light in the middle, which I lit ready for ten o'clock, the appointed start time.

However, I decided to go back out in the garden, half an hour before the scheduled start time to start my healing prayers.

There followed a succession of these pictures, the results of which overwhelmed me, when I witnessed the actual energy that came into the middle of healing circle. Having sent these images on to Robert Allen, he was totally in awe of them as well.

I didn't know it then, but this would be the start of a very special healing area of my garden. Initially I placed a statue of a Buddha next to the bird table and the bench, and over time, added other knick knacks and spiritual healing ornaments.

It wasn't long after using this special area of the garden for healing purposes that one morning I woke up in the early hours, when as it occurred to me that it would be a good idea to get hold of an old piece of slate. For writing on it healing requests with chalk the energies would then manifest for the person who needed healing at that time. I realized then that if I could take a photo after writing the message, this would be a

good way to get proof on camera of spiritual presence and healing.

I brought my first piece of slate from one of my trips back home to Ireland. Initially the healing idea using the slate was for a family member, who needed healing at the time. It was a natural progression to then open up invitations to followers on my healing page, to offer healing for others in need.

I like to do healing sessions for groups of people. For instance, this photo demonstrates my own healing tribute, as I always like to show love and appreciation for our war heroes, past and present.

Often when I hear of tragic news story, I like to do healing session, as a way to send out energies of love and empathy to those involved. Often these poor souls are caught up in the aftermath of some of these heart wrenching stories that we all seem to see on media and the news on a daily basis.

For one to one healing sessions, using an image emailed by the person in need of the healing I would then place this next to the healing statues, for the healing energies to connect.

I have been amazed at the results and quickly became inundated with further requests. So much so, we couldn't keep up and had to stop doing them.

It was quite an incredible and rewarding experience, with the recipients being amazed at the results and the power of visible healing energies coming out on camera!

When I look back, and recall the many times I have nursed family members, often those suffering from cancer. Having done this in the practical sense, it soon became the natural progression for healing I now do in the spiritual sense.

Not long after these first sessions, with healing in mind, my dear friend Linda asked if I would I be interested in going to visit the Healing Sanctuary of the world renowned Healer, Harry Edwards. It didn't take long to plan the trip to Burrows Lea, in Guildford, Surrey. The sanctuary is dedicated to promoting health and wellbeing through their spiritual healing services.

My first thought as we drove into the beautifully manicured grounds, was the tranquillity I immediately sensed. I could almost feel Harry's presence, as we walked through the stunning rooms adorned with a display of pictures and his personal belongings. To this day his home is still a healing sanctuary, and has been lovingly maintained to keep it in its original style since 1946.

I was sat on my own in Harry's healing room, which I had been advised had also been left exactly in the same way Harry had left it.

I asked Harry out loud if he was aware of our presence. I then took a picture of his portrait on the wall, and when looking back on the photo, it was apparent a large orb came out on his painting. I took a few more and the orb turned purple. I then asked for him to show me he could communicate with me, by moving his energy to the corner of the room. To my absolute astonishment his energy did just that!

I then went to the gift shop and as Linda was chatting to a member of staff, I bought a little picture of Harry Edwards and have never looked back since, as I now use this to help with absent healing.

Little did I know at that time that there would be a link in the future to Harry Edwards, as since having various readings, and being told years ago that my spiritual path would eventually lead me in the direction of doing healing, I passed this off as impossible at the time, as to me this meant I would have to be accredited with lots of various certificates. In my heart of hearts, I have never felt comfortable with exams in any shape or form, so this would have been out of the question!

But as the years passed I realise it is a feeling from deep within that helps with spiritual healing, as I have always been able to sense a deep empathy for other people's feelings.

The photo I took (above) is as a result of doing healing prayers. I wrote a message on the healing slate, as I usually do, requesting from Harry that he gives proof of his presence.

The second photo (below) was taken, after placing the book I bought at the sanctuary on my chair, I then asked Harry for a sign.

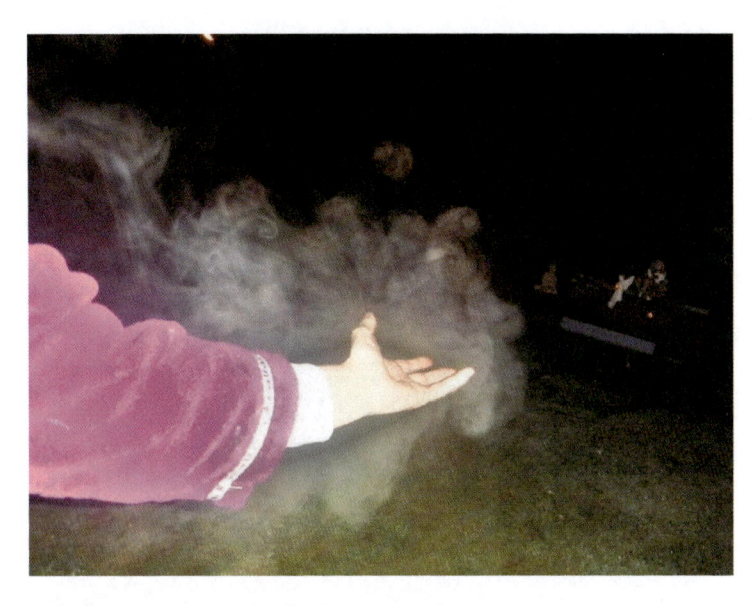

By extending my hand out to spirit, now and again, there has been some amazing evidence returned. They really show they are validating our communication. Sometimes orbs will resonate from the tips of my fingers and travel towards the healing table, thereby manifesting into misty healing energies. This leads me on to some incredible misty images given to me by spirit.

≈Peggy Weber≈

~ - 132 - ~

Healing energies building up once more....

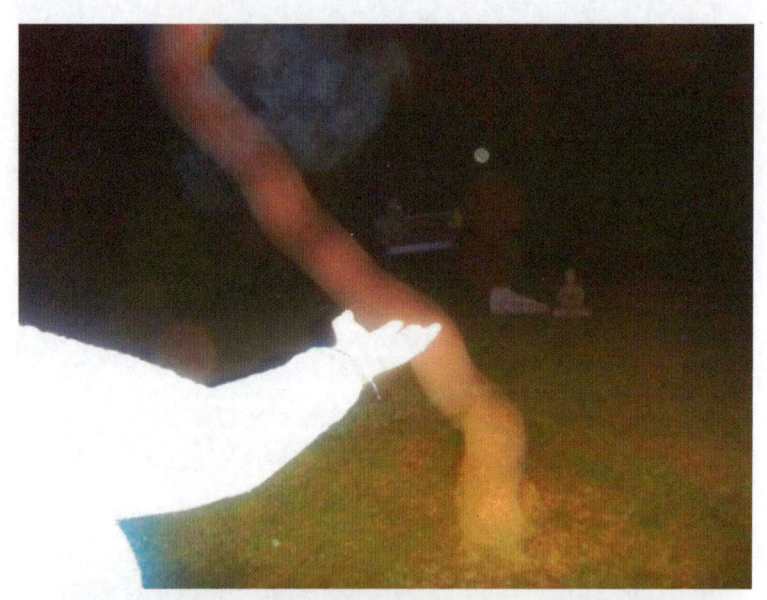

∞CHAPTER 16 ∞

Misty Images

These images that follow, are those I have come to refer to as 'misty' images. They are a manifestation from the orbs. When I take these misty images, each time, definite shapes seem to form incredible images of people, animals, nature spirits and such the like. It is very intriguing that a lot of the misty images I have caught in this way seem to be very similar to those referenced in ancient documented Celtic Symbols. A lot more about will be detailed in my next book.

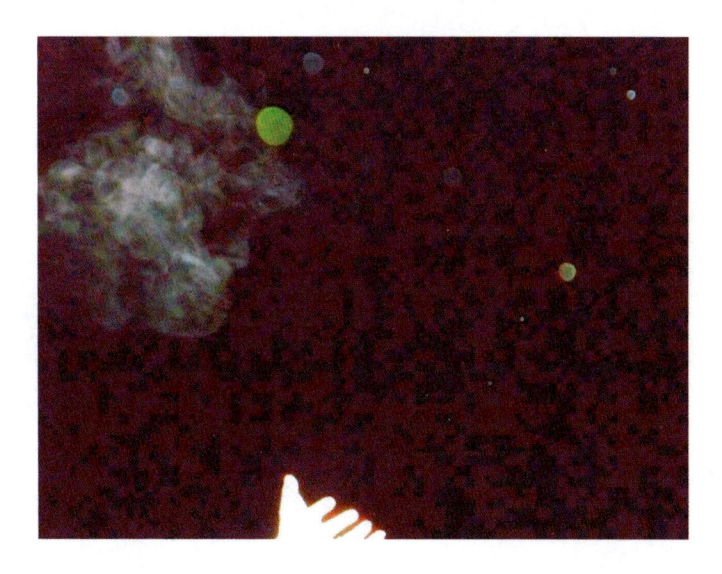

Peggy Weber

This amazing photo above appears to be that of our lovely Irish Setter, Casper, in spirit! The image below is a remarkable image of a wolf head!

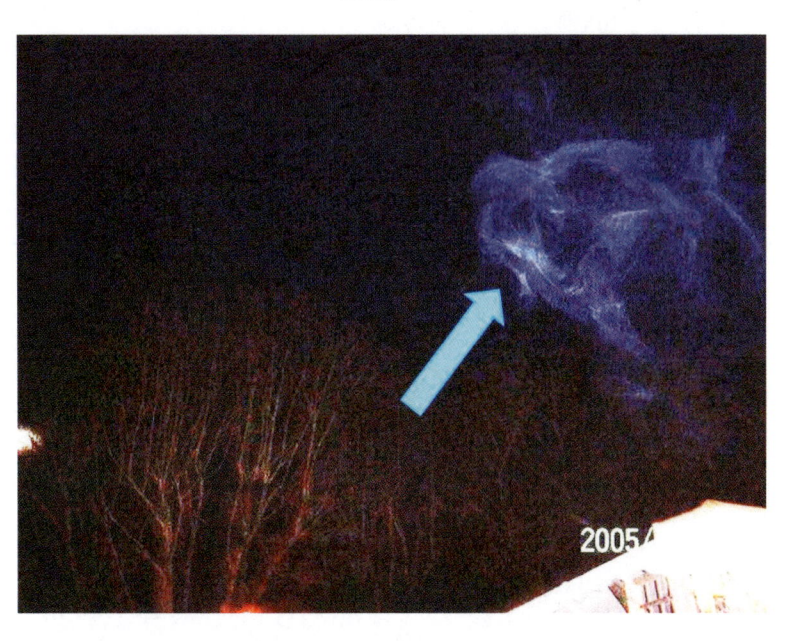

Above is an amazing image, which came out in the clear, albeit, misty image of a Budha for a lovely friend of mine, called Rosemary.

The following photos, firstly shows the image of a bonneted lady! Then the images of our son Paul working on the back of the house. He was a little nervous doing the lighting, and no doubt Tony would have been watching over him! As you can see there is a movement of energy coming to watch over him.

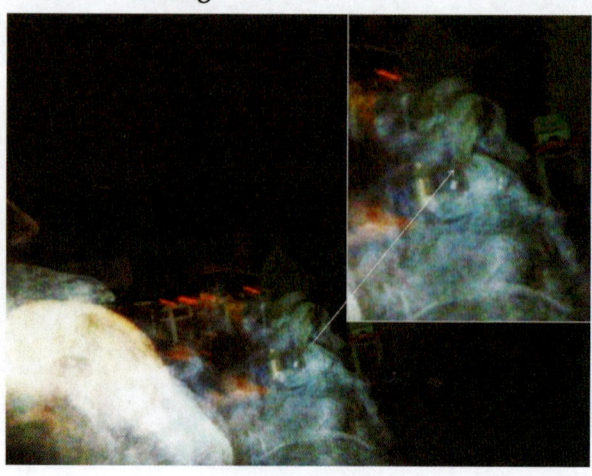

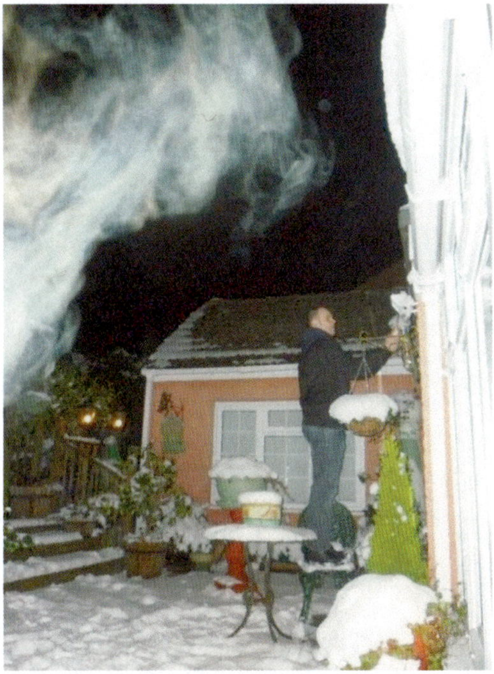

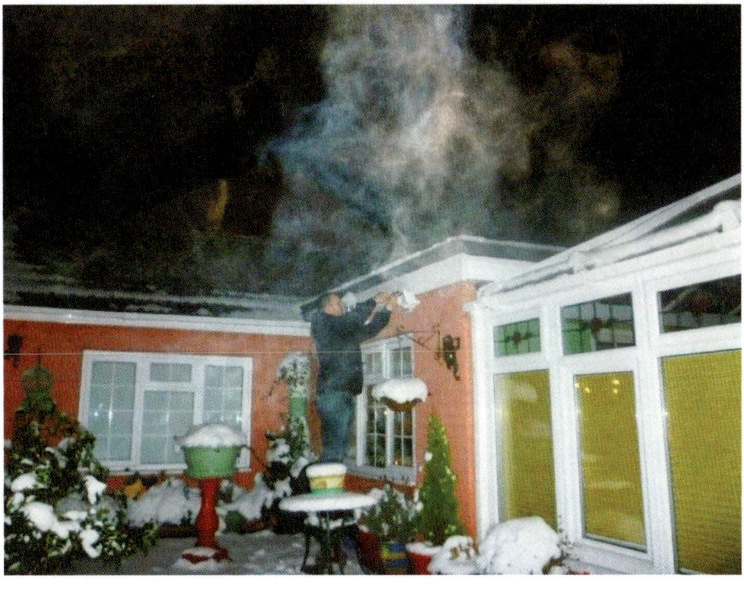

This amazing image of a bearded man standing behind my healing table, was taken during a healing session and just totally amazed me!

❦ TESTIMONIALS ❦

Richard Chelland – Professional Photographer:

"I've not met anyone with such a powerful gift as yourself, the digital pictures you had taken earlier outside Barrington's are just beyond words!

I have studied most forms of psychic phenomena including spirit photography - orbs - earth lights - séance room photography, as my day time job is to manipulate and enhance advertising photography, so with over 30 years of experience I can spot fakes or trick photography almost instantly. Needless to say the digital shots you produced <u>right before my eyes</u> are without doubt the real thing! I'm just staggered by your amazing power! Once again thank you so much for sharing your amazing gift. Truly miraculous!"

Robert Allen – Renowned Healer:

"Some three years ago I was privileged with the true friendship of dear Peggy Weber. She introduced me to her collection of photographs in the realms of healing where the numerous orbs were displayed. Within the orbs it was revealed the content, sometimes Archangels and others where the presence of Angels or Spirit were revealed.

I am but a man of humble healing prayer with the Angels and one evening Peggy and I linked together in healing for those who suffer in any way. She took a photograph in her lovely garden that evening and above her healing ring of daisies was revealed the content of an Archangel watching over. I treasure this photograph and it has inspired me through this validation to continue with evening healing prayers.

How truly Blessed we are to have here on this earth plain the presence of the soul that is our beloved Peggy Weber and long may she continue in her inspirational work she shares with us all."

Reverend Maureen Hinton:

"As a Spiritual Medium myself and Minister of a Spiritualist Church, I have witnessed over fifty years, many instances of spiritual and physical phenomena. I have spoken with many prominent experts on spiritual happenings and I do like to think I have an open mind. I was therefore totally unprepared and only mildly interested when Peggy Weber, walked into our church in 2009, and began to tell me of her interest and work in photographing spiritual orbs. I can honestly say that I was truly amazed and blown away, when Peggy began to demonstrate her great gift before my eyes. Peggy has visited many times over the years since and she is always happy to take time to talk and answer questions for our congregation, whilst always producing amazing evidence. I have witnessed so many incidents, where Peggy would stop whatever we were doing around the church, and begin snapping her camera. The outcome would usually be mind blowing! Peggy is a very humble, honest and unassuming learned lady, with true dedication to her calling, a perfect channel, well chosen for spirit friends to work with.

I count it a great privilege to have met Peggy, I appreciate her great knowledge and I believe she is an important pioneer, who uses modern technology, to further the quest with communication, from the usually unseen world. Thank you Peggy for sharing your beautiful gift with us all. Stand tall in your beliefs always".

✎ SUMMARY ✎

I hope this has been an inspiring and thought-provoking book. It was very hard to choose the right photos, as an introduction to the world of Spiritual Photography (which I have selected from a vast collection I have built up over the years)!

I always get a great feeling of satisfaction to find out I have helped someone in some small way with these images, especially when they are dealing with the terrible grief that comes with losing a loved one to spirit.

Talking of losing family members, it saddens me that nowadays we don't see many of our younger generations attending funerals like they used to. Children are more resilient than we think. As an example of how naturally and innocently kids see things, on the way to my niece's funeral, there was a roaring clap of thunder. The car was quiet, whilst everyone was deep in thought, when little Tony piped up, 'don't worry Mummy, that noise in the sky is only baby Jesus moving the furniture around to make room for Sarah'.

So, somehow in not speaking about life and death at an early age, kids these days only learn about grief, through 'killing each other in electronic games' becoming ever fearful of the 'real' subject area as they grow older, in the artificial world we all find ourselves in today.

There is so much hurt and pain in this world of ours that we thrive on fear instead of the good that goes on. So, if I can help bring even a small amount of comfort, with the knowledge inside this book and sharing the total love intended by spirit, (rather than the way they are often portrayed and misunderstood, through so called Ghost Hunting programmes and the like), I will feel I have helped to pass on 'their' truth.

I really hope my book brings comfort and faith to those who have lost their loved ones, as in my view, and hopefully as demonstrated in this book, they really are still very much with us!

Love and light, Peggy x

ABOUT THE AUTHOR

Born in Kilkenny, Southern Ireland in 1944, Peggy has literally lived with spirit since she was a little girl, in that, not only has she seen spirit with her own eyes, she also captures the images on her standard digital camera!

Peggy travelled to England at just sixteen years old and met her future husband and soul mate and they married in 1965. After having four children, a busy family life meant her spiritual journey had to be paused. Since 2002 Peggy has brought such comfort to so many, during her thought provoking presentations and one to one absent healing sessions. As a result she has given people from all walks of life a new hope, understanding and inner peace when she proves our dearly departed loved ones never actually leave, but connect with us all the time!

Chosen as only one candidate of a possible eight world-wide, Peggy presented her incredible images at The Orbs and Prophets Conference in Palm Springs, USA and again at Glastonbury and across the South East of England, where she has been very well received with her humble, down to earth and humorous nature, not to mention her incredible images of genuine spiritual photography!